SING THE JOYS OF MARY

SING THE JOYS OF MARY

HYMNS FROM THE FIRST MILLENIUM
OF THE EASTERN AND WESTERN CHURCHES

Edited by
Costante Berselli and *Georges Gharib*

Morehouse-Barlow Co., Inc.
Wilton, Connecticut 06897

Original title: *Lodi alla Madonna* published in Italy by Edizioni
Paoline, Roma 1980. Copyright.

Translated from the Italian by Phil Jenkins.

A selection of the hymns from this volume has been published under
the title *In Praise of Mary*, hymns from the first millennium of the
Eastern and Western Churches and 39 matching miniatures.
Also available: *To Him Be Praise*. Hymns to Christ in the first
millennium of the Church.

First published in Great Britain 1982
St Paul Publications
Middlegreen, Slough SL3 6BT, England

First published in the United States 1983
Morehouse-Barlow Co., Inc.
78 Danbury Road
Wilton, Connecticut 06897

ISBN 0-8192-1329-2

Printed in the United States of America

*St Paul Publications is an activity of the priests and brothers of the
Society of St Paul who promote the christian message through the
mass media.*

CONTENTS

FOREWORD

The spirituality and the Christian religion of the times and areas in which the Church, from its beginnings, flourished as a community, and Christianity replacing the earlier beliefs and religious systems, have left a rich inheritance of writing in prose and verse.

The Roman Empire in its largest dimension (about 117 B.C.) included nearly all the Europe of today (with the exception of a good part of Germany and Russia), Asia Minor, Palestine and all North Africa bordering the desert zone.

Over the routes of the Empire the dawning Church found its means of expansion. Over these routes her believers came together in brotherhood, but also suffered inner dissensions and persecutions. These elements, together with the diverse atmosphere of culture and costume, characterised the manifestation of religion, so that, when at the end of the 4th century, the Roman world divided itself into two empires, that of the West and that of the East, the Church also realised the distinctive signs between the communities of the East and the West.

From among these writings in prose and poetry of these first centuries the anthology presents a selection of hymns relating to the Marian cult. It could resemble an archaeological excavation: instead, it reveals exciting important texts for one who is prepared to enjoy them in depth. For this preparation we find helpful the reading of the introduction.

INTRODUCTION

At the beginning of June 1940, by means of radio, at that time the only instrument that allowed one to hear voices from afar, it was possible to listen to a choral prayer, solemnly tragic, soaring beneath the gothic arches of Notre Dame Cathedral in Paris.

It was the whole capital which, in the name of all France, sang the Litany to Mary, under the guns of Hitler's army. It pleaded the intercession of the Virgin through which the French might be spared the horrors which had been the mark of the army sent to oppress and dominate Europe in the name of an ideology which had raised it to the violent symbol of a race, self-defined as the instrument of fate, in order to impose a new conception of life.

Hearing the mournful chant of the Litany suggested the image of a deep pit into which had been thrust those condemned to death, rather than that of a huge basilica; the image and the sound and the dread also involved those not present, to whom the repeated chant of the titles with which they invoked the Mother of Jesus, gave new life to the Christian faith and hope in the face of the calamity which threatened the whole world.

The Litany, a Greek word which means, in a general sense, prayer, is the name reserved for the formula through which the assembly of the faithful unites with the prayer of the celebrant; a formula brought to life again today with the Prayer of the Faithful in the celebration of the Mass.

The Litany most recited in the Western Church is that dedicated to Our Lady and draws its inspiration from the Scriptures and the Fathers, that is, from writers of authority on the subject of faith.

In a manuscript of the 12th century, preserved at Magonza (Western Germany), the Litany is defined as "prayer strongly recommended to be recited in times of tribulation". The author of the first recension of the Litany confirmed the secular method of praying used by the faithful which, invocation by invocation, was probably by anonymous authors; since the Marian cult "forms a very noble part of the whole sphere of that sacred worship in which there intermingle the highest expression of wisdom and of religion and which is therefore the primary task of the people of God". (Paul 6th, *Apostolic Exhortation on the worship of the Blessed Virgin Mary*, 2nd February 1974).

To the Litany of Our Lady, proper to the Western Church, even if its origins were inspired by the prayers of the Eastern assemblies (a Litany, which in the 15th century was called "loretan" for the special place which it held in the public prayer at the Shrine of Our Lady of Loreto) was joined, in the Eastern Church, the *Acathistus*, the liturgical hymn whose title, in its original meaning, indicates that one should stand while it is being sung.

Of the ancient Byzantine hymnology, the authors are not known for certain; leaving it, however, to the critic to designate a preference for one or other of the Greek religious writers, he would not err considering that the compiler had finally edited the hymns and invocations which were already the inheritance of the spontaneous prayer of the faithful. The theme of the *Acathistus* hymn is the Gospel narration which from the Annunciation enlarges on the themes of the incidents relating to Mary and in the enumeration of the blessings received by mankind after the Incarnation of the Son of God. The hymn abounds in poetic images, in gracious titles reserved for the Virgin, proper to the style of feeling and self-expression of the Easterns. As well as is the Litany of Loreto, the *Acathistus*, too, is still sung standing today by the faithful, apart from in liturgical celebrations, in all cases of general calamity. In Paris, in June 1940, the faithful of the Eastern Church would have sung the *Acathistus* beneath the arches of Notre Dame Cathedral.

Litany and *Acathistus* are two examples of spontaneous community prayer, performed by the faithful in the worship of Our Lady, introduced "into the only worship that is rightly called "Christian" because it takes its origin and effectiveness from Christ, finds its complete expression in Christ and leads through Christ in the Spirit to the Father, an indication of the Church's genuine piety". This assertion of Paul 6th, included in the "Exhortation for the Worship of the Blessed Virgin Mary", finds its expression and realisation in the hymns of praise to Our Lady, which have become an integral part of Christian corporate prayer since the end of the first centuries of the Church.

The anthology of hymns presented here is from among the known texts and composed in the first millennium of the life of the Eastern and Western Churches and has the object of making known the sources from which has arisen the Litany and the *Acathistus*. It presents texts, written subsequently, which were inspired by these sources after the communal assemblies lost their initial spontaneity. It was in the middle of the 5th century that it became necessary to propose models for prayers (the first were by Hippolytus of Rome) in which the faithful could be inspired. Models which in a short time became definitive and incorporated into liturgical celebrations.

Mary and the Mystery of Christ, in truth, constituted the first basic subjects of the hymns and of the cult of Our Lady, celebrated with numerous variations.

The theme of the true and proper Mystery of the Incarnation, firmly presented in the Eastern texts, gives the explanation seen through the art, of the widespread cult of icons of the likeness of Our Lady, since the Byzantine spirituality sees in Mary, immaculate from original sin, the first redeemed creature, model of the transformation which is continued in humanity by virtue of the Incarnation of the Son of God the Father.

These explanations at the same time sustain and justify the choice of the hymns presented. They have been drawn from the literary patrimony of the ancient liturgies; Byzantine, Roman, Coptic, Ethiopic, Mozarabic and Gallican and also from the writings of the Fathers of the Church; Eastern-orthodox from Syria, Greece, Egypt and Mediterranean Africa, Ethiopia; Latin-roman from Gaul and Spain, from the period from the 2nd to the 10th century; a living

14

testimony to the Church's spirituality in the various periods in which its expansion occurred.

The hymns, prayers, extracts from homilies and writings intended for meditation and contemplation are included under the generic term of eulogy. As praying is not conveying mental praise and presenting the petition to God, but is, above all, meant to unite thought and feeling to him, free from any rational disturbance and to contemplate the mysteries of faith in simplicity and love.

It was preferred to use chronological order when arranging the selection of these hymns in the anthology. The hymns, appearing in several epochs and over widespread areas, through writers of various origins and social conditions, acquired, therefore, an harmonious progress. There is no subdivision in the way of critical analysis, because the anthology was meant to be a work of popular appeal.

The Italian language in this translation of the texts presented no small difficulty in rendering the spirit of the original writing, either with regard to the literal translation, or with regard to the spiritual mode which the author intends to convey to the reader.

To Hilary of Poitiers (4th century) it appeared difficult to translate into Latin, concepts conceived and expressed in Greek; a language particularly suitable for the subtle distinctions of thought and rich in vocabulary with an abundance of synonyms, though toned down, on the contrary, signifies the distinction between one and the other. Part of this difficulty also occurs in the translation of a text from Latin. The metre and the rhythm are not easy to translate into our languages. However, with an attentive reader, intellectually free from overcriticism, what is not missing is the spirit, the warmth and the theological truth, lyrically expressed; the reader will need to seek them out, collating the texts within the epochs and the neophyte times in which the authors lived.

The liturgical renewal engendered by Vatican Two has endeavoured to bring together liturgical prayer and the spirit of its origins. This renewal will be more thoroughly understood if the expressive formulae of the origins are known and considered.

In particular, with regard to the cult of Our Lady practised as much in Eastern as in Western Churches, these eulogies will help to revivify it within the guidelines clearly indicated by the first Christian communities and by the Fathers who were the inspired teachers of those communities. Later, certain popular forms of the cult of Our Lady, inspired at times by the Marian shrines, were expounded and in most cases accepted, creating their own hymnology which helped to recover the principal dispositions of the spirit free from egoistical changes.

COSTANTE BERSELLI

Costante Berselli was born in 1912. He completed his studies in the diocesan seminary in Mantua. As priest, he spent twenty years in the Curial Office, interrupted in the last year of the war by imprisonment and internment in Dachau Extermination Camp. From 1968, for ten years, he has broadcast on Italian Radio.

NOTES
ON THE PRAYERS TO OUR LADY IN THE EASTERN CHURCH AND IN PARTICULAR IN THE BYZANTINE CHURCH

The prayer to Mary in the Eastern Church originated and was developed with the feast consecrated to her.

Before the Council of Ephesus, we find Mary honoured in the celebrations of two christological solemnities: that of Christmas, the 25th December and that of The Presentation of the Lord, Candlemas (= The Meeting: between Jesus and Simeon) on the 2nd February. The homilies inspired by the christological cycle of Christmas and pronounced between the second half of the 4th century and the beginning of the 5th century make obvious the attempt to institute one single feast in which the essential theme is the Virginal Divine Motherhood, an attempt realised by the Byzantine Church with the institution of the Feast of the 26th December called Synaxis (= Commemoration) of the Most Holy Mother of God.

The Council of Ephesus in 431 in condemning Nestorius and in defending the dogma of the Divine Motherhood of Mary (Theotokos) was decisive for the Marian cult. Churches were founded in Jerusalem, Bethlehem and Nazareth in memory of the principal events in the life of Mary, which was followed by the institution of a cycle of Marian feasts, arising in this chronological order:

6th century:

— Birth of Mary on 8th September;
— Entry into the Temple on 21st November;

— Annunciation on 25th March;
— Dormition or Assumption on 15th August;
— it is also possible to place in this century the development of the theme of Mary's lament, incorporated on Good Friday.

7th century:

— The Feast of the Conception of Anne on 9th December (that which became the Feast of the Immaculate Conception on 8th December in the Latin Church);
— The Feast of Acathistus on the fifth Saturday in Lent.

8th century:

— The Deposition of the Mantle of Mary in the Church of Blachernae (in the North West district of Old Constantinople) on 2nd July;
— The Consecration of Mary every week on a Wednesday.

In successive centuries the cycle of the Marian Feasts acquired a few variations with the addition of the feast honouring Icons and the extra-ordinary festivals of Our Lady, of local character.

With the introduction of new feasts, Our Lady assumes a position ever more conspicuous in the liturgy and in the doctrinal expositions of writers.

The Eastern Church possesses a rich patrimony of Marian texts, still partly in manuscript. The most interesting homilies are traced back to the period from the 4th to the 9th centuries. They were read during the liturgical celebrations by bishops or monastic superiors. Later, to write a homily and read it became almost a fashion, exercised by all, so that not only bishops, priests and monks, but also erudite lay people, and above all, the Byzantine emperors, contributed a considerable number of them. We quote several more well-known names of deliverers of homilies: Basil the Great († 379), Athanasius of Alexandria († 373), Gregory of Nyssa († 395), Anphilochius of Iconium († after 394), John Chrysostom († 407), Cyril of Alexandria († 444), Proclus of Constantinople († 446), Crispin of Jerusalem († 479), Abraham of Ephesus († after 550), Anastasius of Antioch († 559), Sophronius of Jerusalem († 638), Andrew of Crete († 740), Germanus of Constantinople († 733), George of Nicomedia († after 880).

Many of these writers are to be found among the authors of the hymns of praise collected in this anthology.

The hymns, in effect, have literally invaded the Byzantine Office, constituting three quarters of the liturgical books. In the beginning they were brief formulae, meant to be sung by the people between verses of the psalms, an element almost exclusive to the primitive office. However, they became lengthened, multiplied and hidden in every corner of the Canonical Hours, changing their name according to the position they came to occupy in the Office. The Byzantine melodies did not have recourse to the ancient classical metres, but invented a simpler system, based on the tonic stress (omotonía) and on the number of syllables (isosillabía), which allowed the people to sing the sacred text with ease.

The position held by Our Lady in hymnography is copious; not only are the hymns of the feasts celebrated in her honour consecrated to her, but also many of the hymns reserved to the feast in honour of Christ and the saints.

The Marian hymns of the Greek Church reproduced in this anthology come from official books, like the *Horologion*, which contains the formulae determined by the Canonical Hours; the *Triodon*, with the Divine Office of the Lenten season and of Holy Week; the *Pentecostarion*, which links together the Divine Office of the Easter period: the Menaion, six or twelve volumes with the Daily Office of the Saints.

We conclude with a quotation from Vatican Two which, speaking of Eastern liturgical worship, writes: "In this liturgical worship the Easterns glorify Mary, Ever Virgin, with splendid hymns, solemnly proclaimed Mother of God by the Ecumenical Council of Ephesus, because Christ, consistent with Sacred Scriptures may be recognised, in a right and proper sense, as Son of God and Son of Man" (*Decree on Ecumenism*, 3, 15).

(These notes have been edited by George Gharib who also skilfully selected the choice of the hymns of praise belonging to the Eastern Church for this anthology).

Georges Gharib born in Damascus in 1930 is an Archimandrite of the Secular Clergy of the Byzantine Rite under the Greek Melchite Patriarchate of Antioch. He is secretary to the special Liturgical Commission of the Sacred Congregation for the Eastern Church, to which he is also a consultant. He is also teacher of Byzantine Liturgical Mariology and of Moslem Marian Doctrine at the Theological Pontifical Faculty "Marianum" in Rome.

THE MAGNIFICAT

The *Magnificat* (Luke 1:46–55) is a prophetic hymn springing from the heart of Mary on the day on which she visited her cousin Elizabeth. Together with the *Benedictus* of Zechariah (Luke 1:67–79) it became, quite early, part of the so-called *Canticles* or *Biblical Odes*, which, together with the Psalms, constituted almost exclusively the basic principle of every Divine Office of the Byzantine Church.

Over the centuries it has inspired hymnological composition called *megalinaria*. Therefore it seems opportune to introduce this collection of ancient hymns to the Virgin with the one which the Evangelist Luke has handed down as God's inspiration to Our Lady. It is the *Te Deum* of the Incarnation. [Acknowledgement is made to The Grail, England, for permission to reproduce their translation of the Magnificat.]

1. My soul glorifies the Lord,
    my spirit rejoices in God, my Saviour.
    He looks on his servant in her nothingness;
    henceforth all ages will call me blessed.
    The Almighty works marvels in me.
    Holy his name!
    His mercy is from age to age
    on those who fear him.
    He puts forth his arm in strength
    and scatters the proud-hearted.
    He casts the mighty from their thrones
    and raises the lowly.
    He fills the starving with good things,
    sends the rich away empty.
    He protects Israel, his servant,
    remembering his mercy,
    the mercy promised to our fathers,
    for Abraham and his sons for ever.

ODES OF SOLOMON

Discovered in 1905 by the scholar Rendel Harris, in a Syrian manuscript which is assumed to be of Greek origin, they represent the most important discovery after the Didaché (or doctrine of the twelve Apostles, 2nd century) in the field of primitive Christian literature.
There are 40 hymns which reflect, too, every gnostic idea (namely, a particular interpretation of the presence of evil in the world).
Ode no. 19 is the hymn of the virginal conception of Mary.

2. The Spirit spread its wings
over the Virgin's womb,
and she conceived and gave birth,
and became a virgin mother
with much solicitude.
She was with child, and without pain
a Son was born . . .
a model birth,
she possessed him with strength,
loved him in safety,
guarded him with gentleness,
and displayed him in grandeur.
Alleluia.

HIPPOLYTUS OF ROME

He lived in Rome at the beginning of the 3rd century. A native of the Hellenic Middle East, he was a member of the clergy, working as a preacher and distinguished for his zeal in the struggle against heresy. His scholarship and his haughty rigorism led him to become the leader of a narrow but influential circle of believers which opposed the official Church. The struggle came into the open against Pope Callistus 2nd who was accused of laxity; Hippolytus thus became the first anti-pope. His rebellious behaviour continued under Popes Urban and Pontianus until Hippolytus and Pope Pontianus were exiled by Emperor Maximin the Thracian, to Sardinia. There they were reconciled and died as martyrs. His writings (in Greek) are dogmatic, exegesic and of polemic discipline. His main work is *The Apostolic Tradition*, one of the first examples of liturgy containing the formula and directions for the celebration of various Christian rites.

3. O God, we thank you
through your beloved Son,
Jesus Christ
who, when the time was ripe,
you sent to us, as Saviour,
Redeemer and mouthpiece
for your purpose.
He is your indivisible Word,
through which you created the universe
and in which you placed your love.
You sent him from heaven
into a Virgin's womb.
Conceived within her womb, he became flesh
and revealed himself as your Son,
born of the Spirit and the Virgin . . .

HILARY OF POITIERS

Born in Poitiers, in France, to an illustrious pagan family, he had an excellent classical education. He was baptised late, and although already married, about 350 was elected bishop of his city. Stubborn opposition to Arianism made him unpopular with the Emperor Constantius who, in 356, banished him to Phrygia in Asia Minor. From there, Hilary continued to defend orthodoxy, and came into contact with Eastern theology and the study of doctrinal texts. Banished, too, from Phrygia, he returned to Gaul to his episcopal see, where he continued his enlightened opposition to Arian heresy. He wrote the *Treatise on the Trinity*, a *Commentary to the Gospel of Matthew*, a *Comment on the Psalms* (in 12 volumes) and numerous other texts in defence of the faith. His works reveal the depth of thought in which reason and faith unite, in spite of the difficulty of using the Latin language to express theological doctrine, originally discussed in Greek, a language more suitable than Latin to express subtle shades of thought. Some hymns, even if obscure and contorted, open the period of Latin hymnography.

4. How can we so fittingly exchange
an honour so great
so full of love?
The only Son of God,
begotten of unutterable divine origin,
taking shape in the womb of the Holy Virgin,
grows into the form of a human being.
He who holds all
and in whom and for whom
all things exist
was born
according to the laws of human nature;
the One at whose voice
angels and archangels tremble,
heaven and earth
and all the elements

of this world dissolve,
the Invisible One,
He who cannot be incapsulated in any human reality,
He whom we cannot see,
feel or touch,
behold him in his crib, in swaddling clothes.
The person who reflects on these things,
unworthy of a God,
will feel the more for being loved
just because they are in contrast
with divine grandeur.
He, by means of whom
man was made, had no need to become man;
while it was vital to us
that God should become man
and live in us;
that is, by taking on humanity,
he should live within us.
His humiliation is our greatness,
his degradation is our honour;
on the one hand, God was born a man
on the other, the antithesis,
we were reborn in God.

SIBYLLINE ORACLES

The Sibylline Oracles are 14 books of didactic poetry in Greek hexameters, dating from the 2nd century, which include Hebrew and Christian elements. Books 9 to 14 were discovered in 1817 by Cardinal Angelo Mai, paleographer and erudite humanist.

5. He came from heaven
took mortal form.
To Gabriel was first revealed
the one most chaste and true;
Thus spoke the archangel
to the maiden:
"Receive, O Virgin,
the Lord in your Immaculate womb".
At these words
the Lord gave grace to her
who was to be for ever Virgin.
She, hearing these words,
was filled with wonder and with dread.
In stillness she stood trembling
bewildered, as one lost,
the while her heart did throb
to hear the wondrous news.
Then jumped her heart with joy
to find comfort in those words.
She smiled, with blushing cheek,
delighting in her joy,
heart filled with gentle modesty.

And courage came again
and soared the Word within her womb.
He would in time be flesh
and taking life within the womb,
assume the form of mortal man
and be born a child, a child of virgin birth.
This is a great marvel for humankind.
But nothing is too great
for God the Father and for God the Son.
For the new-born Babe
the joyous globe bore wings,
the heavens smiled and the universe rejoiced.
And a star appeared, a star divine,
by the Magi held in awe;
the Infant, swathed in swaddling clothes
was in a manger shown to the followers of God:
watching herdsmen, shepherds of the flock.
And Bethlehem, by will divine,
was called: birth place of the Word.

ATHANASIUS OF ALEXANDRIA

He was born in Alexandria in Egypt in 295. He distinguished himself by defending the Catholic Faith against the Arians, considered to be followers of Arius who deemed Jesus to be inferior to God, and therefore not actually God. At the Council of Nicea in 325 which he had attended as secretary to the Bishop of Alexandria, Athanasius commanded respect for his clarity of doctrine and strength of faith. In 328, on the death of Alexander, he was elected bishop of his city, and remained so until his death in 373: a period of 45 years of toilsome and courageous episcopate, in between flights, persecutions and numerous periods of exile as a result of the intrigues of the Arians. He bequeathed many works in defence of his faith in the divinity of Christ, works in which Mary is always exalted as the Mother of God. In a booklet, written in Coptic, which is attributed to him, Mary is presented as a model for every Christian virgin. The eulogy which follows is taken from a Coptic homily on the *Virgin Mary, Mother of God and dwelling of God,* given by him on return from his second exile, and preserved on a papyrus in the Museum of Ancient Egypt in Turin.

6. O Virgin, your glory transcends all created things.
What, in effect, compares to your nobility,
O Mother of God the Word?
To what in all creation will I compare you?
Angels of God and archangels are sublime,
but how much you transcend them, O Mary!
Angels and archangels in trembling serve him
who lives within your womb,
and venture not to speak;
you, on the contrary, speak freely with him!
We say that cherubs are sublime,
but you are more sublime than they:
cherubs support the throne of God,
you, on the contrary, support God within your arms.
Seraphs are close to God,

but you are closer than they:
Seraphs hide their faces with their wings
unable to look at the perfect glory,
you, on the contrary, not only contemplate his face,
but caress him
and suckle his holy mouth.

GREGORY OF NYSSA

Younger brother of Basil the Great, he was born in Caesarea of Cappadocia (now Kaisarieh in Turkey) about 335. Gifted with acute intelligence and encyclopaedic scholarship, Gregory was, however, lacking in practical perception. This makes clear the difficulty that he had in administrating the diocese of Nyssa of which he was elected bishop.

Philosopher and theologian, he was acclaimed "pillar of truth" at the Second Ecumenical Council in Constantinople in 381. He died in 395. Gregory wrote theological, exegesic and ascetic works of high quality, discourses and homilies. The extracts which follow are passages from two different homilies on the Annunciation, which recent critical sources attribute to him: the first is included in the homilies of John Chrysostom, but this is said to be not authentic; the second was examined and published for the first time in 1909.

7. The angel comes to Mary, and entering, says:
Hail, o full of grace!
In an instant he exalts the maiden and treats
her as a woman,
for she has become the mother of the Lord.

Hail, o full of grace!
Your ancestress, Eve, transgressing,
was condemned to bear her sons in pain.
You, on the contrary, he fills with joy.
She gave birth to Cain
and with him, envy and death.
You, on the contrary, beget a son
who is for all the source of life incorruptible.

Hail, therefore, and rejoice.

Hail, the serpent's head is crushed.

Hail, o full of grace!

For calamity is at an end,
corruption is dissolved,
all sadness now has ceased,
joy has flourished,
the glad tidings of the prophets
have come to pass.
The Holy Spirit foretold,
speaking through Isaiah's mouth:
Behold, a virgin shall conceive
and bear a son.
You are this Virgin.

Hail, then, o full of grace!
You are the delight of him who has created you . . .
You are the delight of those who rejoice in the beauty
of the soul;
you have found a spouse who protects your virginity
leaving it undefiled;
a spouse who, out of such great love,
willed to become your son.

The Lord is with you!
He is in you and in every place,
he is with you and of you . . .
The Son in the bosom of his Father,
the Only Begotten Son in your womb,
the Lord, in the way known alone to him,
all in everyone
and all in you!

Blessed are you among women!
For you have been placed above all virgins,
for you have been found worthy
to give shelter to the Lord,
for you have received within you the One who is
    so great
that nothing in the world could him contain,
you have received him who fills all with himself,
for you have become the place
in which has come to pass salvation,

for you have been the vehicle that has ushered in
the King to life,
for you have appeared as a treasure, a spiritual pearl.

Blessed are you among women!

8. Come, people, let us all sing
of him who is born of the Virgin . . .
let us take courage and, led by the voice of the angel,
thus acclaim the Holy Virgin:

Hail, o full of grace,
the Lord is with you!
To you is gladness due
for the Lord of all
has dwelt in you
in mysterious way which he alone does know.

Hail, o full of grace,
the Lord is with you!
no worldly spouse,
but the Lord himself is with you,
the father of chastity, the guardian of virginity,
he who sanctifies and makes incorruptible,
he who gives freedom and salvation,
and is the governor of peace;
the Lord himself is with you,
for in you is placed the grace divine.

Hail, o full of grace,
the Lord is with you!
Adam no longer has to fear
the one whom he deceived,
for the One who is born of you
has destroyed all the power of the enemy.
The human race no longer has to fear
the deceit and shrewdness of the serpent,
for the Lord has crushed the serpent's head
in the waters of baptism.
I no longer fear to hear: you are dust

and to dust you will return:
for the Lord in holy baptism
has erased from me all stain of sin.
I weep no more, I grieve no more,
nor do I speak:
In my pain, I do not twist in piercing thorns,
for the Lord has taken the thorns from our sins
crowning his own head;
my sin has vanished,
my old calamity dissolved,
the tree of life and grace
flourishes through the Holy Virgin . . .
In effect, the Holy Virgin became for us
the source of life;
source of life for those who believe in Christ,
being the point from which flows
spiritual light.

Hail, o full of grace,
the Lord is with you and of you!
he who is perfect in holiness,
and in whom dwells the fullness of divinity.

Hail, o full of grace,
The Lord is with you!
He who sanctifies all
is with the handmaid of the Lord, with the Immaculate;
he who is the greatest among the sons of man
is with the most beautiful one,
to save mankind, created in his image . . .

c

BASIL THE GREAT

Basil (330c–379) figures as a great bishop of the Eastern Church. He, too, was born in Caesarea, being the older brother of Gregory. Baptised at the end of his studies, he became a monk. Ordained priest by Bishop Eusebius, he succeeded him in the administration of the diocese of Caesarea. While still alive he was named "great" for his various activities as bishop, preacher and a talent for liturgical and monastic organisation. He left a vast and rich amount of literary work, dogmatic and ascetic writings, discourses and homilies, and in addition, letters and prayers including the liturgy which is named after him and which is still used today in the Byzantine Church.

The first extract we quote is a passage from *Homily on the Holy Generation of Christ*. The second is a prayer that Byzantine liturgical books attribute to the saint. It is addressed to Christ, but the invocation is for the intercession of Our Lady. Simple in its brevity, it bears witness to the faith in the powerful help of Mary, in the realm of the cult of saints.

9. O man, know then that God became flesh.
And where did this incarnation take place?
The body of a Holy Virgin!
Let us, too, burst forth with voice of joy.
Let us call our rejoicing theophany.
Let us celebrate the mystery of the salvation of the
        world,
the birthday of mankind.
Today the blame of Adam is revoked.
No longer: "You are dust, and to dust you will
        return";
But, closely united to the celestial world,
you will be lifted even into heaven.
No longer: In pain you will bear sons;
but: blessed is the one who has borne Emmanuel
and blessed the womb that nourished him.

Thus: a babe was born to her,
a son was given to her,
the government is on his shoulder.
My heart revives, my soul exults;
but my tongue is weak and incapable
of announcing a joy so great.

10. You who radiate light and cause the sun to shine
on the righteous and the unrighteous, on the wicked
and the good;
you who herald the dawn and lighten the earth,
O Lord of all, lighten too, our hearts.
Grant that this day that our acts may be pleasing
to you;
defend us from the arrows that fly by day
and against all hostile powers.
Intercede for us, O Immaculate Lady,
Mother of God . . .
For in your might, O our God,
show us mercy and save us.
We give you glory:
Father, Son and Holy Spirit,
now and always and for ever and ever.
Amen.

EPHREM SYRUS

He is the greatest of the Fathers of the Church in the Syrian tongue. Preacher, poet, exegete and controversial writer he came to be called "lyre of the Holy Spirit". Born in Nisibis (now Nisaybin in S.E. Turkey) about 306, he was ordained deacon in 337 and remained one until his death in 373. He left an enormous amount of literary works; his poems in the Liturgical Books of the Syrian Church are famous. They appear in the shape of *Midrash* or poetic homily, which celebrates the mystery of Christ and of Our Lady. Jerome related that Ephrem's works came to be read in various churches after the reading from the Holy Scriptures (*De viris illustribus*, 115).

To select a few texts from the immense Marian works of Ephrem is a difficult undertaking. We present two of them: the first, coming down to us in Greek, sings the praises of Mary becoming aware of the salutation of the angel; the second reflects Elizabeth's salutation to Mary.

11. Hail, song of cherubs
    and angels' praises.
Hail, peace and joy
    of the human race.
Hail, garden of delight,
    Hail, o fuel of life.
Hail, bulwark of the faithful,
    and port of the shipwrecked.
Hail, reminder of Adam;
    hail, ransom of Eve.
Hail, fount of grace
    and immortality.
Hail, temple most holy,
    hail, throne of the Lord.
Hail, o chaste one, who have crushed
    the serpent's head
    hurling him into the abyss.

Hail, refuge of the afflicted,
   hail, ransom of the curse.
Hail, O Mother of Christ,
   Son of the Living God,
   to whom shall be glory, honour,
   adoration and praise
   both now and for ever and everywhere;
And for ever, Amen.

12. *Blessed are you*, O Mary, daughter of the poor,
Who became Mother of the Lord of kings.
In your womb he has dwelt
in whose praise the heavens are full.
Blessed be your breast, which has nourished him
   with love,
Your mouth which has lulled him
and your arms which have held him.
You have been a vehicle to bear a God of fire!

Blessed are you, O Mary, you have become the home
   of the king.
In you he who gave power has taken abode,
who rules the world.
You came from the tribe of Judah;
you descended from the family of David.
Illustrious is your lineage.
For you, though remaining virgin,
have become the mother of the son of David.

Blessed are you, o maiden, who have borne the lion cub
spoken of by Jacob! . . .
He humbled himself . . . and became a lamb,

destined to ascend the Cross to deliver us.
He prefigured you, the tree which providing the kid,
spared the life of Isaac.

Blessed are you, o blessed, since through you
the curse of Eve has been revoked.
Thanks to you, the common debt has been paid
owed to the serpent for generations.
You, in effect, have borne that treasure
which has filled the world with all succour.
From you has come the light which has destroyed
the reign of darkness.

BYZANTINE DIVINE OFFICE

The invocations which follow are taken from the Byzantine Divine Office and are amongst the oldest prayers that have come down to us. In one the *Sub tuum praesidium* is recognised (text discovered in Egypt on a papyrus, probably dated 3rd century) and in another, the *Ave Maria* (discovered in this form in Egypt on an *ostrakon* or fragment of potsherd of the 5th century).

13. Virgin Mother of God,
  Hail; full of grace,
  the Lord is with you.
  Blessed are you among women
  and blessed the fruit of your womb,
  for you have borne
  the saviour of our souls.

14. In the shadow of your mercy
  we shelter, O Mother of God.
  Do not ignore our supplications
  in our temptation,
  but deliver us from danger,
  o pure one, blessed one.

THE SCROLL OF RAVENNA

Discovered in 1833 in the Archives of Prince Anthony Pius of Savoy by scholars A. Ceriani and G. Porro of Turin, the scroll is a tattered parchment which measures 3.60 metres in length and 19 centimetres in width. Written on both sides, the obverse contains Latin liturgical prayers, while on the reverse side are two letters exchanged between a bishop of Ravenna and Sergius, Pope between 900 and 910.

The scroll comes from the Ravenna Church and contains 40 prayers — authentic gems of liturgical inheritance — thought by some to have been used in the main Canonical Hours of Advent. The exegesis of prayer formulae reveals the thematic link with some prayers of early Roman liturgy (4th-5th century) appropriate to the birth of Our Lord. The prayer formulae, which probably originated at different times, and dictated by different authors, go back, according to the most informed critical sources, to the Churches of the Padua area, in a chronological span from the end of the 4th century to the beginning of the 5th century.

15. O God, who in the fullness of time
have revealed the splendour
of your radiant being
through the motherhood
of the Holy Virgin,
so that, to dispel the shadow of sin
truth shines with endless light,
give us, we pray you,
the power to adore for ever
with faith intact and humble demeanour
the mystery of such an incarnation,
and to exalt it with pious homage.

16. Eternal God and creator of life,
who by the coming of the birth of Christ
took flesh,
we pray to you that he
be full of mercy
to us, his humble servants;
he, the Word, came to us
from the womb of the Holy Virgin
to become flesh
and dwell among us.

17. O, God, eternal majesty,
your unutterable word
pronounced by the angel
was received
and the immaculate Virgin
became the dwelling of the living God,
filled with the light of the Holy Spirit;
we beg of you that she,
who was worthy to bear
in her holy and chaste womb
the Christ, God and man,
may protect with her intercessions
her faithful people.

18. O true light, our Lord God,
who from the depths of your heart
have voiced the saving Word,
we pray to you:
as wondrously you descended
into the pure womb of the Virgin Mary,

grant us, your servants,
to await with joy
the glorious nativity.

19. O God, who in the Virgin's womb
with wondrous art,
have made
a holy dwelling in the flesh:
come, you righteous one,
come swiftly
and, according to the ancient promise,
ransom man from his plight.
To you let there rise up the praise
worthy of so great a love
and to us be given eternal salvation.

20. O Lord, O God,
the virginal dwelling
is at last ready in all its beauty,
so that, to celebrate the royal nuptials,
the bridegroom is enticed
the finest among the sons of man;
in his fullness, he would give peace and joy
to all people
and with his enlivened presence
the shadows will finally be dismissed
from our souls.

GALLICAN LITURGY

It was in use until the 9th century in the Latin West, especially in Gaul. The Gallican Rite declined under Pepin the Short and Charlemagne as a consequence of the progressive Romanisation of Gaul pursued by Carolingian politics. In general it was more solemn and complete than the old Roman liturgy because of its external ceremonies and for the style of the prayers. There remains, therefore, a precious record of the religious atmosphere as lived in the Church north of the Alps.

21. It is truly suitable and wise,
 just and beneficial
 to give thanks to you, almighty and eternal God,
 that Jesus Christ, our Lord,
 has come upon the earth.
 Through love, from heaven he descended,
 emerged from the sanctuary of the Virgin's body.
 Scarce he appeared as Saviour of humankind
 than did the angels sing "glory in the highest heavens"
 and they exulted
 for earth had received the King of ages.
 Mary, the blessed one, became the precious temple
 to keep watch o'er the Lord of lords.
 To cancel out our sins
 she begot Life sublime;
 and Life vanquished bitter death.
 The womb that knew no human blemish
 was worthy shelter for the Lord.
 Born into the world is he
 who lived in heaven for ever
 and still in heaven lives.

JEROME OF STRIDO

He was born in Strido in Dalmatia (347) and completed a normal course of studies at Rome. Difficult and restless by nature, from Rome he went to Trier, Aquileia and Antioch (where he was ordained) to Constantinople and finally to Bethlehem, where he died in 420. He is well-known for his translation of the Bible (Vulgate version) into Latin from the original Hebrew and Greek, and for his letters (154), rich in learning and a witness to his life and the history of his time. They are held by scholars to be written in wonderful style. His Marian doctrine is outlined in some polemically apologetic works (*Against Jovinian, Against Elvisius*) and in various sermons and commentaries.

22. "Let the peoples honour you, O God,
let all the peoples honour you".
we said it once
and were not heard;
we repeat it, so that you may acclaim it . . .
Why do we insist again?
"the earth has given its fruit".
The earth: Holy Mary,
who sprang from our world
and from our lineage . . .
This earth has given its fruit,
and finds in its Son
what was lost in Eden.
"The earth has given its fruit".
First, it gave the flower . . .
the flower became a fruit
for us to eat,
and be nourished by it . . .
The son is born of the Virgin,
the Lord of the maiden,
God of humankind,
The Son of the Mother,
the fruit of the earth.

ACATHISTUS

This hymn, composed between the 5th and 6th centuries, is so-called because it was sung "standing" which is the meaning of the Greek word. It is without doubt the most famous hymn to Our Lady in the Byzantine Church; as popular among the Christians of the East, as the Rosary is in the West. It is a literary masterpiece of theology, highest expression of contemplation and praise to the Virgin Mary.

The hymn consists of 24 strophes or stanzas, corresponding to the letters of the Greek alphabet. The first 12 stanzas, of historical character, are based on the Gospel Infancy; the other 12, of strictly theological character, expound the major Marian themes.

23. Hail, you who carried in your womb
　　the guide for all who stray,
　　Hail, you who have borne
　　the deliverer of servants;
　　Hail, appeaser of the just judge;
　　Hail, pardon for those who have repented;
　　Hail, refuge for those who despair;
　　Hail, love which surpasses all desire;
　　Hail, chaste spouse!
　　Wondering at the birth unearthly
　　we become strangers to the world
　　turning our thoughts to heaven . . .
　　. . . the Most High
　　as a poor man appeared upon the earth,
　　wishing to raise on high
　　all those who proclaim:
　　Alleluia!
　　The coming of God to earth
　　did not admit a change of place;
　　The Son was born of the Virgin,
　　and, in welcoming her God,
　　to her ears came the words;

Hail, seat of the infinite God,
Hail, gateway of majestic mystery;
Hail, unheeded warning to the unfaithful;
Hail, sure pride of believers;
Hail, most holy vehicle
of him who stands above the cherubim;
Hail, perfect dwelling
of him who stands above the seraphim . . .
All the company of angels
were stirred by the grandeur of
the Incarnation.
They saw God inaccessible
become a man accessible to all
and stand among us to be
received by all:
Alleluia!
We see superb orators
become mute like fish,
O Mother of God.
They are unable to explain how
you still remain a virgin, though having given birth.
On the contrary, we place our joy
in the contemplation of the mystery,
we proclaim with faith:
Hail, dwelling of the wisdom of God,
Hail, treasure of providence,
Hail, you show the ignorance of scholars,
Hail, you reveal the pride of orators,
Hail, because the discerning reasoners have
become fools;
Hail, because the poets of the myths have waned;
Hail, you who smash the pagan fallacies;
Hail, you who fill the fishermen's nets;
Hail, you who raise us from the depths of ignorance;
Hail, you who have made the truth shine to so many;
Hail, haven of so many who long to be saved;
Hail, port of the navigators of this life;
Hail, chaste spouse!
The Creator of all things,

wanting to save the world,
of his own will came into the world.
He, God, although our Shepherd,
for us appeared among us as a man.
Having thus called us all together,
He, God, listens:
Allelulia!
You are the protector of virgins,
O Virgin Mother of God,
and of all who turn to you.
The Creator of heaven and of earth
made you thus immaculate,
to dwell within your womb
and to teach all to sing to you:
Hail, pillar of virginity;
Hail, gateway of salvation;
Hail, initiator of new issue,
Hail, manifestation of the divine goodness,
Hail, you who have given new life
to all who were begotten in sin;
Hail, you who have restored right thought
to those deprived of understanding;
Hail, you who discomfit those who pervert minds;
Hail, you who breed those who foster chastity;
Hail, nuptial bed of chaste marriage;
Hail, you who united believers with the Lord;
Hail, sweet educator of virgins;
Hail, o you who adorn the holy souls
through mystical marriage;
Hail, chaste spouse!
Every hymn must fail
that attempts to equate
your infinite mercy, O God.

If hymns we were to sing to you,
as many as grains of sand, O King,
never could we match the worth
that you have given us,
for we proclaim:
Alleluia!

ANONYMOUS HYMNS

In the following anonymous hymns (dating between 5th and 6th centuries) to be found in the Book of Hours of the Greek Church, there are once again Marian themes of preceding centuries, but in a more moderate and concise form, where the hymns end in a cry for help and supplication. It is a prelude to the flourishing hymnography of the following centuries.

24. We salute you, O Virgin Mother of God,
Impregnable wall and strength by which we are saved.
You scatter the counsels of adversaries,
turn into joy the sorrow of your people,
make the world hear your voice,
strengthen him who is devoted to you,
intercede for peace upon earth.
You are, O Theotòkos, our only hope.

25. We, the people of all nations, proclaim
you blessed, O Virgin Mother of God;
He who surpasses all things,
Christ, our God, in you has deigned to dwell.
Blessed are we, who have you as our defence,
for you intercede night and day for us . . .
And so we hymn our praise to you, proclaiming:
"Hail, o full of grace, the Lord is with you!

26. What shall I call you, o full of grace?
I shall call you Heaven: for you have caused
the sun of justice to rise.
Paradise: for in you
has bloomed the flower of immortality.
Virgin: for you have remained inviolate.

Chaste Mother: for you have carried in your arms
a Son, the God of all.
Pray to him to save our souls.

27. O Mother of God, you are the true vine
which gives the fruit of life.
We supplicate you: intercede, O Lady,
Together with the apostles and all the saints,
That God should have mercy on our souls.

28. Since we have no trust in ourselves,
by reason of our sins,
plead with him who is born of you,
O Virgin Mother of God.
The prayer of a mother can do much
to secure the goodwill of the Master.
He indeed, is merciful
and can deliver us,
He, incarnate, who accepted
to suffer for us.

29. A thousand times glorified are you,
O Virgin Mother of God!
We hymn our praise to you, for by the Cross
of your Son
hell has been overthrown
and death humiliated;
we, who were dead, have been revived
and made worthy of life;
we have gained paradise,
our principal reward.
Therefore, we glorify you, O Christ our God,
the almighty and merciful one.

CYRIL OF ALEXANDRIA

He was the greatest Egyptian Father and Doctor of the Church (Alexandria 370–444), the most prolific writer of the East after John Chrysostom. His characteristics are clarity and depth of thought. He was considered the theologian of the Mystery of the Incarnation and the vigorous defender of the Divine Motherhood of Our Lady. He confronted the heretical patriarch Nestorius and the doctrine was solemnly confirmed by the Council of Ephesus in 431. It was on that occasion that he made the most famous speech of ancient times in honour of the Mother of God.

30. Hail, Mary, Mother of God,
sacred treasure of the universe,
inextinguishable flame,
crown of virginity,
sceptre of orthodoxy,
indestructible temple,
tabernacle for him
whom the world could not contain,
Mother and Virgin!
Thanks to you, the Gospels praise
him who comes in the name of the Lord.
Hail, you whose virgin's womb
contained the sublime.
Thanks to you
the Cross is venerated
and adored throughout the world;
the heavens exult,
angels and archangels are joyful,
the devils are pursued,
the wicked tempter falls from heaven.
Thanks to you, debased humanity
has been to heaven raised,
and all of those beings subject to idols,
reached cognition of the truth.

Through you the holy baptism
is the oil of delight for the faithful;
Through you there are so many kinds
of churches in the world,
through you people gather together in unity.
And what more should one say?
Through you, the light, the only begotten Son of God,
shone on those who lay
in darkness and the shadow of death;
through you the prophets predicted the future;
the apostles announced salvation to the people;
the dead rise again . . .

PROCLUS OF CONSTANTINOPLE

He became Patriarch of Constantinople in 434 in a difficult period in the life of that Church, still troubled by Nestorius's heresy. His literary work includes homilies and letters, but lacks precise outline. The discourses attributed to him that have come down to us show us a distinct oratory, modelled on the school of John Chrysostom. A great defender of the Divine Motherhood of Mary, his hymns to Our Lady inspired the unknown author of the Acathistus hymn. He died in 446.

31. The Holy Mother of God has called us here together,
the Virgin Mary, the Immaculate jewel
of virginity,
the paradise of the second Adam,
the place of the union of nature (human and divine)
of coming together and linking
the shrine of marriage between Word and flesh.
the thriving bush which the fire of a divine birth
did not consume,
the truly light cloud
which carried, united in one body,
the one who is seated above the cherubim,
the purest fleece from the heavenly rains
with which the shepherd reclothed the lamb.
Mary, maiden and mother,
heavenly Virgin,
the unique bridge between God and mankind.
The great and marvellous loom of the Incarnation
on which was ineffably woven
the tunic of union,
in which the Holy Spirit was the weaver,
virtue, the spinner, foretold from on high,
wool, the ancient fleece of Adam,
weft, the immaculate flesh of the Virgin,
shuttle, the immense grace of the one whom

she assumed,
craftsman, in the end, the Word which entered into her
to hear what she ascribed to the Word.

32. Let us admire today a group of women:
let us acclaim Sarah, honour Rebecca,
let us admire, too, Leah, and praise Deborah.
And let us call Elizabeth blessed.
And let us venerate, too, Mary, for she became Mother;
She, maidservant, cloud, nuptial bed and ark
of the Lord.
Mother: she bore indeed
the One who chose to be born into this world.
Maidservant: acknowledged nature, preached grace.
Cloud: conceived indeed by the Holy Spirit
him whom she bore without corruption.
Nuptial Bed: In her, indeed, dwells the Word of God
as in a nuptial abode.
Ark: not because she contained the law,
but because she carried the legislator in her womb.
Let us acclaim, therefore: blessed are you among
women!
You, the only one who has lightened the pain of Eve,
the only one who wiped away the tears of one who
mourns,
the only one who bore the redemption of the world,
the only one to whom was entrusted the treasure
of the precious pearl,
the only one who without pleasure of the senses
became pregnant
and without pain gave birth,
the only one who begot Emmanuel
in the way he chose.
Blessed are you among women
and blessed is the fruit of your womb.

THEODOTUS OF ANCYRA

Theodotus, Bishop of Ancyra in Galatia (now Ankara, capital of Turkey) lived in the first half of the 5th century, and was one of the most convinced defenders of the Divine Motherhood of Mary. Six homilies attributed to him in which Mary occupies a position of affectionate regard, have come down to us. We select an excerpt from the 4th homily.

33. Let us be guided by the words of Gabriel,
citizen of heaven, and say:
Hail, O full of grace, the Lord is with you!
We say again with him:
Hail, O our such longed for joy!
Hail, O rapture of the Church!
Hail, O name so full of fragrance!
Hail, O countenance illuminated by the light of God
from which such beauty flows!
Hail, O memorial full of reverence!
Hail, O spiritual and salutary fleece!
Hail, O bright mother of the dawning light!
Hail, O stainless mother of saintliness!
Hail, O gushing fount of living water!
Hail, new mother and moulder
of the new-born One!
Hail, O inexplicable and mystery-filled mother!
Hail, O new book, a second Isaiah;
Book of the new Scripture
in which the faithful witnesses were angels and men!
Hail, O alabaster vase
of holy ointment!
Hail, you who give honour to virginity!
Hail, O humble space, which welcomed to itself
Him whom the world cannot contain.

ESICHIUS OF JERUSALEM

Born in the last decade of the 4th century, he became a monk
and then a priest in the Church of Jerusalem. He was an impas-
sioned commentator on the Bible and a theologian. Numerous
writings are attributed to him, including some well-known
Marian homilies. We select the following hymn from the 2nd
homily on the Mother of God (sermon no. 5).

34. Every grateful creature feels it must greet
the Virgin and Mother of God,
imitating, as much as possible, Gabriel,
prince of the angels,
who says: hail!
who proclaims: the Lord is with you!
for the sake of the Lord who became flesh in you
and appeared to mankind.
who calls her: Mother of light,
star of life.
Some call her; throne of God.
Others: great temple of heaven.
One: a seat not inferior to that of the cherubim;
Yet another: virgin and fertile garden,
vine of fine grapes, flourished and untouched,
pure turtle dove, chaste dove,
uncorrupted cloud, filled with rain;
jewel case, whose gem shines more brightly than
    the sun;
quarry, from which has been hewn, without cutting,
the stone which shelters all the earth;
vessel without steersman, charge of precious things;
treasure which grows rich.
Yet others call her:
Lamp without a wick, which burns by itself;
ark, more spacious, longer, more noble
    than that of Noah.

BASIL OF SELEUCIA

He lived at the time of Monophysite crises (the Monophysite heresy maintained that in Christ there was but a single nature) and vigorously defended the true Faith, confirmed by the Council of Chalcedon in 451. He died in 459. He left homilies. We give an excerpt in which Mary is exalted, stressing her faith.

35. O most Holy Virgin,
    he who gives you venerable and glorious titles
    does not fail to tell the truth,
    on the contrary, it falls short of your worthiness.
    Look on us benevolently from heaven!
    Govern us with peace;
    guide us, without intimidating us
    before the judge's throne;
    and make us worthy to be seated on his right,
    to be transported to heaven
    and to become, with the angels,
    the cantors of the eternal Trinity,
    known and glorified, in the Father, in the Son,
    and in the Holy Spirit.
    now and always
    and for ever and ever. Amen.

BALAI

A poet of the Syrian language, he died about 460. He was probably responsible for the Church of Berea, now Aleppo in Syria. A very prolific lyric poet, he left numerous poems, many of which are included in the liturgical books of the Syrian Church.

36. Blessed are you, O Mary,
    because in you are fulfilled
    the mysteries and enigmas of the prophets.
    Moses offered you in the burning bush
       and in the cloud,
    Jacob, on the ladder which rose to heaven,
    David, in the ark of the covenant,
    Ezekiel, in the closed and sealed door.
    Here their mysterious words
    are realised in your birth.
    Glory to the Father who has sent his only Son,
    That he should show himself through Mary,
    should liberate us from sin,
    and his name should be glorified in heaven and
       on earth.

AUGUSTINE

Born at Tagaste in 354 (now Souk-Ahras, in Algeria), he converted at the age of 33 after a long cultural and spiritual struggle which is testified to in his *Confessions*, and was baptised in Milan by Ambrose. Augustine, who became a priest and bishop of the city of Hippo (now Bona) is, and remains, the powerful mind that brought together the values of the civilisation of his time, of which he was a skilled judge. Philosopher and theologian, and interpreter of the most profound themes of the faith, and the defender of orthodoxy against various heretical attacks (by Bishop Donatus, the monk Pelagius and others), he was a pastor particularly conscious of the ministry of the Word and bequeathed more than 800 sermons. He died in 430. His literary activity was the most copious of all Roman antiquity and occupies 15 volumes in the Migne *Patrologia Latina.*

37. Christ is born:
   God from the Father,
   man from the mother.
   From the immortality of the Father,
   from the virginity of the mother,
   from the Father without a mother,
   from the mother without a Father;
   from the Father beyond time,
   from the mother without seed;
   from the Father as the beginning of life,
   from the mother to put an end to death . . .
   We still cannot contemplate
   the offspring of the Father
   before the morning star;
   we celebrate his virgin birth
   in the dead of night.

38. Lord, you deigned to become flesh,
The Word made flesh;
Word above us, flesh before us;
The Word made flesh, place between God and man.
You chose a Virgin through whom you were born
  and became flesh;
You found a Virgin who would conceive;
and you left her a Virgin
after your birth.

39. Who are you that with such faith have conceived
and soon is to become a mother?
The One who created you will be born in you.
Whence came to you such great goodness?
You are virgin, you are holy . . .
Much it is you have merited,
or better, much it is you have received!
He who created you has become incarnate in you:
the Word of God,
through whom the heavens, earth
and all things were made;
The Word, not ceasing to be God,
assumes in you the nature of a man,
becomes man . . .
When he was conceived, you were a virgin;
a virgin still, when he was born.
It seems an indiscretion
that I question thus the Virgin
and so disturb her reserve.
But the Virgin, blushing yet, to me replies:
"You ask whence came to me such goodness? . . .
Listen to the angel's greeting
and believe in the salvation which comes from
  my womb;
Believe in him in whom I have believed".

MOZARABIC RITE

The Mozarabic Rite, also called Visigothic or Spanish, draws on the Latin literary culture of Visigothic Spain of the 7th and 8th centuries, surviving until the 12th century. Full of clear concepts with magnificent cadences, it is now only preserved at Toledo Cathedral.

40. It is a worthy, just, suitable and salutary thing
to celebrate the wondrous coming
of Jesus Christ, Our Lord,
which the heavenly messenger announced
must be born amongst men and for men;
whom the Virgin welcomed on earth
while she was being greeted
and through the Spirit was made flesh,
since, through Gabriel's promise,
through the faith of Mary
and the concurrence of God's spirit,
the event would follow the greeting of the angel,
the fact would show the fulfilled promise
and the Virgin would understand
that she would be a fruitful bearer
of the mysterious power of the Highest.
The angel announced: "Behold, you will conceive in
   your womb
and will give birth to a son",
"How shall this be known?" asked Mary.
But she asked, believing, without doubt;
The Holy Spirit then accomplished
that which the angel had announced.
Mary, virgin before her conception,
and who remained a virgin after the birth,
conceived her God
first in her mind, then later in her womb.

The Virgin, filled with the grace of God,
first welcomed the saviour of the world
and therefore became the true Mother of the Son
    of God,
adored by the angels . . .

SEDULIUS

Probably born in Italy, date uncertain, he would have spent part of his life in Greece. He was a priest and probably a bishop. He was, with Prudentius, one of the most read and the most imitated of all the poets of the 5th century. He left four books, entitled *Paschale Carmen* which recapture in detail the outline of an epic rendering of Holy Scriptures: the ancient Covenant, the life of Christ, his miracles, his Passion, Resurrection and Ascension. His lyrical form is sincere, his creative force remarkable. He died about 449.

41. As much light upon the earth,
as there is grace in all the heavens!
What splendour
when Christ came forth from Mary's womb
such glory had never been seen!
He was like a bridegroom
who comes exulting from his nuptial bed of glory,
handsome with an attractive beauty,
not ordinary like that of man;
radiant is his figure
and on his lips
is seen a gentle grace . . .

Hail, Holy Mother,
who has given birth to the King;
He who governs heaven and earth
in time
and whose divinity and whose dominion,
— which do for ever all embrace —
are without end.

Your blessed womb has given you the joy
of motherhood and the honour of virginity;
you are like one who has no equal
among women, before or after you;
You are the only woman, unique and beyond compare,
who was pleasing to Christ.

42. From the East
Unto the ends of the earth,
let us sing of the sovereignty of Christ,
born of the Virgin Mary!

Mighty creator of all things,
he wished to reclothe the nakedness
of the mean body
so that, through the flesh,
he might free the flesh
and so might deliver from perdition
those to whom he had given life.

The celestial grace
entered into the womb of the Virgin Mary.
The maiden carried in her womb
a mystery unknown to her.

The sanctuary of a pure body
unforeseen, becomes a temple for the Lord.
An untouched virgin brought forth a Son . . .
The One whom Gabriel had foretold
And whom John, still in his mother's womb,
had acknowledged.

It befell him to lie down in the hay,
he did not scorn a manger.
He who provides nourishment for the birds,
was himself fed on a little milk

The heavenly choir rejoices,
and the angels of God raise their song.
To the shepherds
the Shepherd reveals himself, creator of all things.

MAXIMUS

He is the first bishop of Turin to be recorded by name (4th-5th century). He developed as a pastor through the works of Ambrose (in the works of Maximus there are a good 77 quotations of the Bishop of Milan). He was full of zeal and paternal solicitude for his people. His discourses give us a marvellous moral portrait of him which makes up for the lack of precise biographical data. Between the barbarians hammering at the gate (the first invasion into Piedmont by Alaric's vandals was in 402) and the dying civilised Roman world, Maximus found himself obliged to undertake social and political duties together with those of a priest. Strong, and a sure leader of his people, Maximus, with his pithily expressed discourses reflects the religious and social conditions of the times.

43. It is necessary that the Saviour
born of a Virgin without blemish
would be received by an uncorrupted heart:
and as Mary bore him chastely,
so does our soul
guard him without sin.
Mary is the model for our souls.
Since Christ,
as he sought the virginity of his Mother,
thus entirely seeks our souls.

44. In Christ there was no thorn of sin
to turn into a flower;
Since he was the flower
born not of a thorn, but of a branch,
As the prophet said: "he will come forth from
   a branch
of the stem of Jesse
and a flower will sprout from its roots".

The branch was Mary,
tender, sincere and virgin
who bore Christ like a flower
through the integrity of her body.

AMBROSIAN HYMNS

Evidence going back to the earliest times testifies to the first Christians' custom of accompanying their sacred meetings with the singing of hymns. Extracts from the lyrical passages found in the Holy Scriptures, especially in the Psalms, were used as the text for these hymns, but gradually original compositions appeared. Ambrose, Bishop of Milan, is looked upon as the true inventor of sacred hymnology in the West, having introduced into the liturgy the singing of hymns which he composed, not based on sacred texts. Following him, there was a flourishing of hymns which, alike in scale and structure to those of Bishop Ambrose, were generically termed "Ambrosian" and came to form almost a *genus*, a literary form to this day. The popularity enjoyed by them tends to make one neglect the names of the authors. It is not, therefore, an easy task to identify the writings of Ambrose in these chants. Augustine gave evidence of the authenticity of four of the fifteen hymns as certainly being those of Ambrose. Among these there is the *Intende qui regis Israel* (which we present) for the feast of Christmas. In it appears the Mother of God, delicately praised.

45. Turn to us, you who lead Israel,
You who are seated above the cherubim;
you who appeared in the presence of Ephraim,
revive your power and come!

Come swiftly, Redeemer of humankind.
Manifest the One who is born of the Virgin.
Let all ages admire him!
Such a birth becomes God.

Through a mystical breath of the Spirit,
not from human seed,
The Word of God became flesh;
the fruit of the womb ripened.

The womb of the Virgin enlarges
but the cloister of modesty remains intact.
The standards of the virtues glitter.
Christ dwells within his temple.

Let him come forth from the chaste and regal womb,
as from his nuptial bed,
the Most High God-man
to briskly run his path.

He came from the Father,
returned to the Father,
descended into hell, ascended to the throne of God.

You who are equal to the eternal Father,
clothed yourself in our flesh
to strengthen with unfailing vigour
the feebleness of our body.

Resplendent is your manager;
the night irradiates its light;
let no shadow darken it
but always shine with the light of faith.

PETER CHRYSOLOGUS

A native of Emilia-Romagna (probably of Imola) he was elected
Bishop of Ravenna about 425, under Valentinianus 3rd and
Galla Placidia; he was a friend of Popes Sixtus 3rd († 440)
and Leo the Great († 461). From his numerous sermons we can
draw outstanding elements of Christian life in Ravenna at the
beginning of the 5th century, and in particular, information on
the celebration of the Eucharist and on the liturgical year. In
his sermons, dealing for the most part with the mystery of the
Incarnation, he frequently recalls the Mother of God.
He was nicknamed Chrysologus, namely "golden-worded". He
died about 458.

46. Truly blessed is the Virgin,
  who possesses with the decorum of virginity,
  the dignity of Mother.

  Truly blessed,
  for she was worthy of bearing the son of the
    All-Highest;
  and kept the crown of blameless virginity;
  received the glory of the divine issue,
  remaining the chaste queen of virgins.

  Truly blessed,
  for she was greater than heaven,
  stronger than earth,
  wider than the universe.
  She who welcomed in her womb
  the One whom the world cannot contain,
  the One who rules the universe,
  She became mother of her creator,
  nourished him who sustained all living things.

47. Virgin,
it was not nature but grace that made you mother;
love willed that you should become mother . . .
With your conceiving, with your giving birth
modesty has increased,
chastity, integrity and virginity
have been strengthened . . .

Virgin,
if all remained untouched,
what have you yielded?
If a virgin, how are you a mother?

Virgin,
he, thanks to whom
everything that is in you has increased,
nothing in you has diminished.

Virgin,
your Creator was in you conceived;
from you is born the source of your being;
he who brought light to the world,
is brought forth from you in the world.

PRUDENTIUS

A Christian Latin poet, born in 348 in Calahorra (Spain). He was a rhetorician, and private counsellor to the Emperor Theodosius; retiring from public life, he began the "new life" of a poetical career, diverse and fruitful. His poetry, lyrical and didactic, is like a little liturgy which the poet celebrates for himself and for his readers. To his vast learning, classical, biblical and poetic, Prudentius adds the sincerity of a religious fervour, and above all, the vital force of an imagination ever inspired by Scripture, doctrine and events. A kind of Christian Baroque resembling the formal style and the dazzling colour of mosaics and of contemporary frescoes. In the *Hymns for the Day* the Daily Hours are put into verse, from "cockcrow" to "slumber"; others are for the period which goes from Lenten fasting to Epiphany. He died about 405.

48. A new line will appear
from another man, come from heaven
and not like the first one, from the mire;
he is true God, of human nature
but without the imperfections of the flesh.

The Word of the Father becomes living flesh.
Let the blameless maiden give birth to him
who is the shining God,
no human connection
has made her fruitful.

An old hate antagonised
man and the serpent,
the origin of the future victory of Our Lady.

Then the serpent, crawling on the ground,
was trampled on by the feet of Our Lady;
The Virgin, indeed,
who was deemed worthy to bear God,
triumphed over all evil.

70

Fruitlessly coiled up upon itself,
the serpent spits out impotent venom,
mingling its colour with the green of the grass.

PAULINUS OF NOLA

Paulinus, a native of Bordeaux (France) of an illustrious and rich Roman Christian family, studied under renowned teachers and enjoyed a political career. With the approval of his wife he distributed his immense wealth to the poor when he was baptised in 396. Later he became Bishop of Nola in Campania; he was the cantor of the miracles of St Felix, near to whose tomb in Nola, he retired. His poetry also brought together some detailed compositions that "christianise" the habit of scholars of embellishing, with short narrative poems, even the smallest event in life (352–431).

49. God created the holy maidservant
like the interior courtyard of a temple,
respectfully surrounded by reverence,
open to the rain and the dew.
Then he himself descended from the clouds of heaven
on silent wing, soft and humble,
as once the dew fell upon Gideon's fleece.
But no-one has succeeded
in penetrating the mystery, fulfilled
in the silent way
of God, become man in the womb of a virgin.

O profound zeal of the Lord for the salvation
    of man!
The Virgin offers herself for the son
without the collaboration of man;
sublime mystical image
for the marriage of the Church with Christ!

She, too, is indeed a sister of the Lord
and loving wife; and as mother
she receives the seed of the eternal Word,
carries the people in her womb
and gives birth to them.

The spouse whom no-one has touched,
truly remains the sister of love;
her embrace is the Spirit,
for the one who loves her is God.

ELEUTHERIUS

Born in 456, he was probably the first Bishop of Tournai (a Flemish city, already important in the 4th century and later capital of the Kingdom of the Franks) in a troubled era, with the political horizon obscured through the downfall of Roman power and the invasion of the Franks. Neither the numerous anecdotes, related in the story of his life, nor all the works attributed to him (*Sermons, Profession of Faith, Prayer to the Virgin*) are proved by textual critics. He died about 531 and his body is preserved in a beautiful sarcophagus in Tournai Cathedral.

50. O angel's salutation,
full of sweetness and joy!
Saying "Hail, Mary"
he offers to the Virgin
heaven's salutation.
Saying then "full of grace"
he declares the punishment pardoned
for which the ancestors
were estranged from God
and proclaims restored
the gift of celestial blessing . . .
O blessed Virgin,
O Virgin, selected and predestined
by the creator of the world,
mother, without meeting man,
you will conceive the One
who, before all ages,
was begotten without mother
of the eternal Father.

51. O Virgin,
give us not only food for the body,
but also the bread of angels

come down into your virginal womb.
Make us fear the Son of God . . .
for he who fears God will keep his commandments
and purify his senses
so as to gaze on the splendour of divine light.
After we have been granted
purification of the senses
there will follow enlightenment
of the heart.
Hear us then, O Virgin benign,
and receive our prayers.
O Virgin . . . pray to God for us
that he will grant us perseverance,
and the strength to endure,
that peace may be strengthened
and love increased;
so that when the day comes
of sorrow and misery,
of calamity and sadness,
you will deign to present us
to your only Son,
who alone is God . . .
Amen.

JACOB OF SARUG

He was Bishop of Batna, a small town near Edessa in Turkey.
He wrote various theological and poetical works, through which
he was compared with Ephraem Syrus, and in whose footsteps
he followed in promoting Marian doctrine. He was also called
"the Flute of the Holy Spirit" and the "Lyre of the Orthodox
Church". He died in 521 and is venerated as a saint among the
Jacobites, the Maronites and the Armenians.

52. O Mary, you are blessed among women
and full of riches . . .
pure Virgin and mother . . .
cloud of mercy,
who bears the hope of all the world.
Through you the whole afflicted world
    was given peace;
vessel of riches, through means of which
the treasure of the Father
was sent on earth to rich and poor;
field which has yielded a harvest
without the work of a plough;
and this harvest has satisfied the hunger
of the whole world.
Untouched vine, which though unpruned, has given
    grapes,
whose wine, see, uplifts the sorrowing world;
daughter of the poor, mother of the only rich one,
whose treasures, see, abundantly enrich beggars.
Letter in which was written the mystery of the Father,
who through your flesh appeared to the world,
so that the world might be renewed.
O letter, they did not write and thus did not seal;
but they sealed it and then wrote it;
what a miracle!
Since after it was sealed, it was written mystically,

and without being opened, was clearly read;
it was a letter, and that which was written was the
    Word,
and when it was read, it was renowned through
its forecast to the world.
It sank into insignificance, for it was simple,
but it did not lose its greatness
for it had been honoured.

THEOTEKNO OF LIVIA

He lived between 550 and 650 and was Bishop of Livia (a
small town in Palestine, not existing today). He was author of a
homily on the Assumption of the Virgin Mary, recently discovered in a manuscript in the Sinai. In this homily he affirmed
his belief in the mystery of the bodily assumption of Mary into
heaven.

53. Let us rejoice with the Mother of God,
    unite in the chorus of angels
    and celebrate this feast of feasts:
    the Assumption of the Ever-virgin.

    On earth she was the treasure and the model of virgins;
    In heaven she is as one who intercedes for all.
    Favourite of God, procuring for us the gifts of the
      Spirit
    and with her word teaches wisdom.

    The ever virgin Mother of God, our earth blossomed.
    While she was on earth, she watched o'er all,
    She was like a universal providence
    for all the faithful.
    Ascended into heaven, interceding for us,
    she became a secure refuge for the human race,
    near to her Son and God.

PSEUDO-ATHANASIUS

This was the title of the unknown author of a homily on the Annunciation included in the works of Athanasius which critics, however, after about three centuries, subsequently deemed to be that of the Patriarch of Alexandria. He died in 373.

The excerpt which we translate is a laudatory paraphrase of the angel's salutation.

54. Remember us, most Holy Virgin,
still virgin after the birth.
Grant to us, through these humble supplications,
the great gifts from your rich treasure, O full of grace!
As a worthy celebration of praise,
our hymn and that of all creatures
would rise to you, O full of grace,
Mother of God and ark of holiness.

Our first hymn would be that
which the archangel addressed to you, exclaiming:
Hail, O full of grace, the Lord is with you!
All generations shall call you blessed.
The heavenly hierarchy of angels,
together with man, with hands upraised,
will bless you, O blessed in the heavens
and announce thus on earth:
Blessed are you among women
and blessed is the fruit of your womb!
The first hierarchy of the thrones,
the Cherubim and Seraphim, in blessing exclaim:
Blessed are you among women
and blessed the womb which bore God
and the breast which suckled the babe.
The second hierarchy of the Lords,
Power and Might, contemplating you, cry:
Blessed are you among women . . .

So too, the hierarchy of angels and archangels,
through the voice of the archangel Gabriel,
extol in a magnificent and glorious hymn, exclaiming:
Hail, full of grace, the Lord is with you!
And we ... our mouths full of the praise of God,
copy their accents
and glorify you, exclaiming aloud:
Hail, O full of grace, the Lord is with you!

Pray for us, O Lady, O Queen and Mother of God,
for you are of our stock,
and it is God who was born of you
and through you became flesh.

To him be given glory, splendour and honour,
adoration and thanksgiving,
together with his Father,
and the Holy Spirit, good and life-giving,
now and always, and for ever and ever.
Amen.

ANONYMOUS AUTHOR
OF THE 6th CENTURY

55. Mother of God, Virgin, queen of all,
do not ignore us who entreat you,
tossed by the storms of life
and tempted by evil.

O higher than all the powers of heaven,
golden dove of the Spirit,
pride and joy of the apostles,
harmony of the prophets and martyrs,

succour of the whole world,
precious tower, clothed in gold,
city of twelve gates, paradise,
coffer of spiritual unguent.

impregnable rampart, fortress, bulwark . . .
defence of him who is pious and devout,
protection for him who lives in chastity.

We venerate you, ineffable lady,
and praise your son and our Lord,
Christ, unique friend of man,
in order to find grace and love
on the day of judgement, O Lady.

F

THE FEAST OF THE ASSUMPTION
OF MARY

The Feast of the Assumption or the passage of Mary to Heaven, originated in the Church of Jerusalem in the 6th century. The first homily on the feast appears to be that of Theotekno of Livia, dating between 550 and 650. A decree of the Emperor Maurice, about the year 600, directed the celebration of the feast to be on 15th August, in all the churches of his empire.
We translate two short prayers, derived from an older collection from the Byzantine celebration of the Feast of the Assumption.

56. In your Motherhood you preserved your virginity
and in your dormition you did not abandon
    the world, O Theotokos.
You spent your life being mother of Life,
and with your intercessions you liberate our souls
    from death.

57. In your Motherhood, conception had no seed;
in your dormition, death was uncorrupted.
O Mother of God, you experienced a miracle of
    miracles.
In fact, how could a woman who has not known
marriage, nourish at her breast a babe,
though remaining a virgin?
And how does the Mother of God come to be anointed
with spices, as though she were dead? Therefore, we
    cry to you
with the angel: "Hail, O full of grace!"

MODESTUS OF JERUSALEM

He was Patriarch of Jerusalem where he rebuilt the holy places destroyed by the Persians. He died in 634 and is honoured as a saint in the Greek Church.

The prayer which follows is included in an important discourse on the Annunciation, which is attributed to him.

58. Hail, O most holy Mother of God our Redeemer,
who through you came to live with us and we with him;
he who made you worthy to be extolled and venerated
as the true and proper Mother of God,
may you be honoured by many on earth
and above all, by the angels in heaven,
as the most venerable Mother of God.

Hail, O revered and immaculate Mother of God!
he who from the highest heaven, without leaving
heaven,
came into your womb as into his own home,
he the same Christ the Lord, made you worthy of
passing
from this worldly place to the heavenly home,
which he gave, through you, to the saints who him
awaited.

Hail, Mary, splendid spiritual paradise!
You have gathered, through the power of the
Holy Spirit
the fruit of life and of immortality:
the One who was begotten of the Father, Christ
our Lord.
We, partakers of his life through true belief,
in him have been given life.

He built for you, in paradise, a tabernacle,
where you dwell with your glorified body;
through you, for us too, the door is opened.

Hail, O most adorned and shining refuge!
You have been made the Mother of God.
The human race, shipwrecked on the sea of life,
in you is saved;
through you it has obtained the gift of life
from the One who honoured you in time
and glorifies you for ever and ever.

SERGIUS OF CONSTANTINOPLE

Sergius 1st, Patriarch of Constantinople from 610 to 638 — the
year of his death — was of Syrian origin. He helped to save the
imperial capital from the siege of the Avari (a Caucasian tribe)
in 626. On that occasion he introduced the singing of the
Acathistus hymn and created the feast of that name on the 5th
Sunday of Lent. To Sergius is attributed a Contakion on the
Dormition of Our Lady, on the model of the Acathistus, composed of a prelude and 14 strophes, where the angels and
apostles appear who have come to render homage to the
Assumption of Our Lady. We present the last two strophes, in
the words of mankind and the poet.

59.   *Mankind*

O Holy Virgin
who have begotten the Word, in flesh,
bless our souls,
let us live in faithfulness,
we who at all times praise you
and proclaim you thus:
save us, O gate of salvation;
protect us, O mother of truth;
succour the faithful who honour you,
O immaculate;
Save us from the possible, innumerable failures,
O most pure;
protect, defend, guard
those who hope in you.
Free from all temptation
those who have recourse to you.
Break the arrows of the wicked demons;
quench our passions,
poor and worthless mortals.

The Poet
Save him who with faith sings this hymn to you.
Help him to overcome his passions;
entrust him to extol you with fervent love;
accept him who acclaims you so ardently:
Hail, Virgin and spouse!

SOPHRONIUS OF JERUSALEM

He was born in Damascus in Syria in 560. After having travelled widely in the East and to Rome with his friend Moschus, a monk and writer, he was elected Patriarch of Jerusalem. When the Arabs of Caliph Omar besieged the Holy City in 635, and conquered it in the following year, Sophronius undertook patient negotiations to extenuate the grievous consequences of the Arab invasion. He died in 638. He left some homilies, among them one on the Annunciation, from which is taken the eulogy we quote.

60. Hail, mother of celestial joy
Hail, you who nourish in us a joy sublime,
Hail, seat of redeeming joy,
Hail, you who offer us perennial joy,
Hail, O mystical abode of ineffable joy,
Hail, O most worthy place of indescribable joy.

Hail, O blessed spring of infinite joy,
Hail, O divine treasure of endless joy,
Hail, O shady tree of life-giving joy,
Hail, O Mother of God, unwedded bride,
Hail, O Virgin, unblemished after giving birth,
Hail, wondrous vision, far above any other marvel.

Who could describe your splendour?
Who could tell of your mystery?
Who could know how to proclaim your grandeur?
You have embellished human nature,
you have surpassed the angelic legions ...
you have surpassed all creatures ...
we acclaim you: Hail, O full of grace!

ANATOLIUS

A hymnwriter of the 7th century, of whom very little biographical detail survives. Byzantine liturgical books have preserved some hymns which are attributed to him.

61. The archangel Gabriel was sent from heaven
to Nazareth, village in Galilee,
to bear to a maiden an announcement of joy.
And when he stood before her, he exclaimed thus:
Hail, O full of grace, the Lord is with you.
Hail, dwelling place of divinity!
    The One whom the heavens could not contain
    was contained in your womb, O blessed one.
Hail, O delight, salvation of Adam,
    Redemption of Eve, joy of the world . . .
Hail, inflamed throne . . .
Hail, celestial seat of the king;
Hail, untouched mountain, dwelling worthy of every
honour.
    In you, indeed, dwells the fullness of divinity,
    through the will of the eternal Father
    and the intervention of the Holy Spirit.
Hail, O full of grace, the Lord is with you!

ANONYMOUS HYMN OF THE 7th CENTURY

62. Grace of the angels, joy of the afflicted,
mediatrix of Christians, Virgin Mother of the Lord,
protect me and save me from eternal suffering.

Mary, the most pure thurible of gold
has contained the sublime Trinity;
the Father has delighted in her,
the Son has dwelt, and the Holy Spirit,
having foretold to you, O Virgin,
has defined you Mother of God.

We rejoice in you, O Theotokos;
You are our defence next to God.
Stretch out your invincible hand
and crush our enemies.
Send to your servants succour from heaven.

MARY'S LAMENT

The theme of Mary at the foot of the Cross, already outlined by Ephraem Syrus (4th century) rose to a dramatic height under Romanus Melodus (6th century) and found a notable development in the Byzantine celebration of Holy Week, from which are taken the extracts and songs of lament which follow. These 180 elegies on the dead Christ, proper to the morning of Holy Saturday, are divided into three groups or stanzas, dating from the 7th century.

63. You were placed in a tomb,
O Christ who is life,
and the legions of angels, astonished,
glorified your compliance.

The chaste one poured out a mother's
lamentations and tears, O Jesu,
and cried: My Son, how will I be able to bury you?

Like a grain of wheat
planted in the depths of the earth,
you produced an ear of grain, laden with fruit,
making mortals rise again, born of Adam.

The ewe lamb, seeing the death of her lamb,
overwhelmed by sorrow, lamented,
stirring all the flock
to weep with her.

O Light of the world! My Light,
Jesu, my delight!
Exclaimed the Virgin,
in plaintive lament.

O God and Word, my joy!
How will I be able to bear
your sepulchre for three days?
Now my maternal inmost feelings are tearing me.

Who will offer the showers and founts of tears
to weep for my sweet Jesu?
says the virgin spouse of God.

O mountains and valleys,
O multitudes of men, O entire universe,
weep and lament with me,
mother of your God.

When shall I see you, O Saviour,
light without beginning,
joy and delight of my heart,
exclaimed the Virgin, lamenting.

We extol you, O chaste Mother of God;
and with faith we honour for three days,
the sepulchre of your Son and our God.

64. It is right to exalt you who gave life,
you who placed his hands upon the Cross
and crushed the power of our enemy.

Alone among women, O Son, I gave birth
to you without pain;
but now I suffer the intolerable pains
of labour,
wept the holy one.

To restore the broken nature of mortals, O mother,
of their free will they are guilty
of the death of my flesh;
so, do not beat yourself, lamenting.

Your mother offers you the libation
of tears, O Christ,
While, as flesh, you lie in the tomb,
and she cries: Rise again, as you foretold!

Seeing you on the Cross, O Word, pierced by nails,
your mother's soul was wounded
by the nails and darts of a grievous sorrow.

Seeing you as you drank the bitter potion,
you, the sweetness of the universe,
your mother's face is bathed in bitter tears.

I am obviously wounded,
my inmost feelings are tearing me, O Word,
seeing your unjust killing,
said the most chaste one, lamenting.

Set upon the earth, O sun of justice;
for the moon which bore you,
O Saviour, through sorrow has vanished,
taken from your sight.

See the disciple whom you loved,
see your mother, my Son,
and give us your sweetest word,
the chaste one, lamenting, wept.

Alas, Son, wailed the one unacquainted with man,
and said: the one who hoped to be king,
now I see him on the Cross, condemned.

Thus Gabriel announced to me when he descended;
he said the reign of Jesu, my Son,
would be eternal!

Alas, the prophecy of Simeon is accomplished;
Your sword has penetrated my heart,
O Emmanuel!

She wept bitterly, O Word,
your most chaste mother, seeing you
in the tomb, ineffable, eternal God.

65. All generations, O my Christ,
offer up a song at your sepulchre!

Seeing the misfortune of your death, O Word,
the purest one raised a mother's lament,
O my gentle spring, my sweetest son,
where has your beauty gone?

Your most chaste mother, O Word,
laments you, for you are dead.

The heifer wailed
to see her calf hanging on the wood.

She wept, the Virgin, shedding ardent tears,
her heart pierced.

O light of my eyes, o my sweetest son,
how can they hide you now in a tomb?

To free Adam and Eve, O mother,
I suffer this passion, do not weep!

I give glory, my son, to the immensity
    of your mercy,
for which you suffer these torments.

Gazing on your Cross, O Christ,
weeping bitterly, the immaculate mother said to you:
O life, do not tarry among the dead!

In olden days, the whole house mourned the son
    of Rachel;
now the choir of the Apostles, together with the mother
laments the son of the Virgin.

Now you are left to drink vinegar and gall,
O merciful one, to destroy the old inclination.

You have been left, nailed to the gallows of the Cross,
you who once protected your people with a
column of clouds.

Rise again, you who give life,
weeps the mother who bore you.

Hasten to rise again, O Word,
dispel the sorrow of your chaste mother.

Your purest mother weeps and laments
over your death, O my Saviour.

O Virgin, make your servants worthy
to see the Resurrection of your son.

VISIGOTHIC BOOK OF PRAYER

The Book of Prayer included in the treasured Codex 89 of the capitular Library of Verona (discovered by the archivist Maffei in 1732) is, without doubt, the oldest text of the Mozarabic Liturgy. It was used in Spain before the Arab invasion, an epoch to which, undoubtedly, the manuscript has to be attributed. It is assumed, on established grounds, that it originated in the Church of Tarragona; and it is obvious that a codex written in visigothic script belonging to this city, dates necessarily prior to 711, namely to the fall of the city into the power of the Arabs.
A text venerated for its antiquity and valid for the extraordinary richness of its prayer formulae, it is of great importance for its biblical, liturgical, theological and hagiographical content and for its literary form. The manuscript of Verona (large codex of 127 sheets 330 x 260 mm written in tiny visigothic script) contain 1,121 complete prayers, antiphons, responses or similarly short texts written in the margins of the pages.

66. O Virgin,
who, begetting Christ,
have redeemed the human race,
offer to the ear of God
the prayers of those who invoke you.
You, who without corruption,
begot the saviour of all,
intercede for us
and obtain from the Lord,
joy and pardon for our sins.

67. O holy Mother of God
who, receiving the angel's message,
conceived the Word,
you gave your consent in faith,
you begot your Son in the flesh,

deeply disturbed by the divine presence,
but trustful in the help of grace,
receive your people's requests, you who can,
and fully grant the prayers of each one,
so that, welcoming into your maternal womb
all those who, exiles on the journey of life,
take refuge in you with certain hope,
you may present them, saved,
to the Lord Jesus Christ, your Son.

68. . . . You came to us through the Virgin
without violating the gate of her virginity,
neither entering into, nor coming forth from her.
O Lord who can do all things
we implore you with all our strength;
you who granted your Mother
to be both virgin and mother,
through her prayers,
bestow on your Catholic Church
an incorruptible faith and fertile charity;
thus will your Church be able to give birth to
a people of believers
and, freed from all guilt,
she may reach you without spot or wrinkle.

69. Listen, daughter, and behold:
you have become a daughter of your Son,
handmaiden of your child,
mother of your creator,
bearer of the most high Redeemer.
The King has fallen in love
with the splendour of your beauty
and has deigned to prepare for himself,
a most pure dwelling
in his world.
Obtain for us, therefore, from him
who, taken by longing for you,

made you his mother,
to pour into us the wondrous sweetness
of desire for him,
so that we remain dedicated to his service
in this life,
and our journey o'er,
without chaos we arrive
with him who was born of you.

70. O Maiden and most holy Mother of the Word . . .
from the depths of your compassion
welcome the people who have recourse to you.
Nourish, with the outflow of your loving kindness,
the flock which the son born of you
with his blood redeemed.
Offer your bosom to all who are created,
you who nourished the creator of all.
As a reward of service to you
extol all who come to pay their homage.
And we who are happy to serve you
will always be protected
by your mediation.

71. O Christ,
blessed is the Virgin, your Mother,
glorious queen of the world,
for, at the greeting of the angel,
she believed that which was announced
by the Lord would be accomplished.
To us, who do not cease to extol
her virginal conception,
give us, we pray you,
the ability to reach with pure heart
the solemnity of your Birth.

ILDEFONSUS OF TOLEDO

Bishop of Toledo and writer (617–667) he is known as the theologian of the Mother of God for his principal work on the Virginity of Mary, which is at the root of all Marian literature in Spain. He wrote several works of a remarkable theological degree in which the traditional patrimony of the great Fathers is evoked, also a *De viris illustribus* in which he presented 14 personages of the Spanish Church. His mystical and legendary figure inspired the painter El Greco, as well as being the subject of a comedy by Lope de Vega, called *The Virgin's Chaplain.*

72. Hail, O torrent of compassion,
   Mother of God and mother of forgiveness.
   river of peace and of grace,
   splendour of purity, dew of the valleys;
   Hail, only salvation of your children,
   solemn throne of majesty,
   place of shelter, temple of Christ,
   the way to life, lily of chastity.
   Hail spouse of Christ,
   flower of lovable grace,
   humble maidservant.
   Most beautiful and worthy of reverence.
   no other woman was or can be like you.
   We acclaim you: revered one,
   your spirit is pure, and simple your heart,
   chaste is your body.
   You are indulgent and merciful,
   dear to God, beloved above all.
   The person who enjoys you, still ardently desires you,
   still thirsts for your holy sweetness,
   and always unfulfilled, confines his longing
   to loving you and praising you.

97

G

73. Through your grace, O most holy Virgin,
my bonds are loosened,
my debts would be excused,
the injuries I have caused would be remedied.
The ancient man in me would be renewed,
that which is feeble would be strengthened,
that which is in ruins would be restored,
and that which is imperfect would be improved.
Through your goodness,
my will would be strengthened,
my mind enlightened,
my soul inflamed,
my taste sweetened
and my countenance adorned.
Help me, O light that brightens,
O sweetness that would divert me,
O power that would fortify me,
O prop that would support me.
Remove from my lips
every false and evil word,
from my mind every dismal thought.
Let your grace
direct my whole life.
Amen.

GERMANUS OF CONSTANTINOPLE

The Patriarch Germanus (Constantinople 635–733) is a saintly
figure caught up in the iconoclasm of Emperor Leo the
Isaurian, to whose irrational fury he was opposed. Despite his
being 96 years old he was banished to exile. He left nine
homilies, of which seven are on the subject of Mary, of whom
he was a great devotee and zealous apostle. The emphasis he
uses when speaking to the Virgin and to entreat her, was to be
echoed later in the writings of Bernard of Clairvaux.

74. O my sole comfort,
divine dew, refreshment for my thirst,
rain that comes down from God on the dryness of
    my heart,
shining lantern in the darkness of my soul,
guide for my journey,
support for my feebleness,
shelter for my nakedness,
wealth for my extreme poverty,
balm for my incurable wounds,
end of my tears and of my lamentations,
deliverer from all misfortune,
comfort for my sorrows,
deliverer from my slavery,
hope of my salvation . . .
This you are, O my Lady;
this you are, O my refuge,
my life and my help,
my protetcor and my glory,
my hope and my strength.
Grant that I may enjoy the indescribable
and incomprehensible gifts of your Son
in our heavenly home.
You possess, in effect, I am aware,

a might equal to your will,
for you are the Mother of the Most High;
so thus do I dare and confide.
O most pure Queen
may I not be deceived in my expectation.

75. Your help is efficacious, O Mother of God,
to achieve salvation,
and it needs no other commendation
in approach to God.
You, in effect, are the true mother of the true life,
you, the leaven for the renewal of man,
you, the deliverance of Eve's dishonour . . .
No-one obtains grace,
if not through you, who were worthy to receive
God himself in your womb . . .

And through this, with reason, every sorrowing person
turns to you, and the ailing draw close to you . . .

You remove from us scorn and wrath,
the tribulations and temptations of the devil
and divert the righteous ones from the menace
and the judgement of a merited condemnation,
through the great love which you bear
for the people who take their name from you.

Through this, the Christian people,
recognising their unhappy state,
entrust to you with confidence their prayers,
and beg you to present them to God.

Their certain hope is to yield to you
and to obtain their request, O most Holy,
through the happy experience of former times,
and the multitude of your favours lavished upon us,
and imploring you continually,
to urge you to hear us with good will.

For the one who will not call you blessed?
Hardly, in effect, a Christian, he is seized by fear,

and stumbling on a stone, immediately
invokes the protection of your name . . .

We are seized with admiration for you,
O unchangeable hope, firm protection,
secure refuge, ever-watchful protectress,
everlasting salvation, ever-ready succour,
complete protection, impregnable wall,
treasure of delight, irreproachable garden,
secure fortress, fully strengthened moat,
tower of powerful help,
gate through which the tempest has swept,
tranquillity for the one who has a troubled soul,
safety for sinners, refuge of the despairing,
summons to the exiles, return for the expelled,
reconciliation between enemies, condemnation of the
    damned,
blessings to the cursed, dew of the confused soul,
vigour and life of the felled and aged tree.

Through you, in effect, say the Scriptures,
our bones will sprout like grass;
you who are the mother of the shepherd and the lamb
and the declared mediatrix of all good things . . .

ANDREW OF CRETE

He was a monk, orator and hymnwriter (Damascus 660c–
Mitilene 740). First, he was a monk in the monastery of St Saba
near Jerusalem, then a cleric. About 700 he was elected Arch-
bishop of Gortyna on the island of Crete. He took part in the
struggle against the Monothelitist heresy (which confesses only
one will in Christ without distinction between human and divine
will) and in the defence of the cult of Icons. He was, like his
contemporary John of Damascus, a great composer of hymns,
preserved in the liturgical books of the Byzantine Church. He is
said to be the inventor of a series of canons, long poetic compositions divided into nine odes, each of which contains a certain
number of strophes. Andrew of Crete has honoured Mary in
numerous homilies and hymns.

76. Exult, O righteous ones; heavens, rejoice;
mountains, dance for the birth of Christ.
The Virgin is seated, copying the cherubim,
carrying in her arms, God, the Incarnate Word.
The shepherds glorify the newborn One;
the Magi offer gifts to the Master;
the angels, singing, say:
Sublime Lord, glory to you!

O Virgin Theotokos, who begot the Saviour,
you have revoked the curse of Eve,
for you became a mother, carrying in the womb,
with the Father's blessing, God,
Word Incarnate.
The mystery does not allow argument,
with a unique faith we glorify him,
proclaiming:
Sublime Lord, glory to you!

Come, let us sing praises to the Mother of the Saviour,
who remained a virgin after the birth;
Hail, live city of the God-king,

in which Christ has dwelt
and has fulfilled our salvation.
With Gabriel, we praise you
and glorify you with the shepherds, saying:
O Theotokos, intercede with him, to whom
you gave flesh,
and so save our souls.

77. O Virgin, from you
as from an unhewn mount,
Christ was carved, the cornerstone
which has interlinked the divided peoples.
For this we rejoice
and glorify you, O Theotokos!

Come, let us remember with pure heart
and chastened soul, the Daughter of the King,
the splendour of the Church,
more resplendent than gold,
and let us glorify her!

Hail! and rejoice, O Spouse of the great King,
you who splendidly reflect
the beauty of your spouse,
and exclaim with your people:
O Giver of life,
we glorify you!

O Saviour, give your heavenly aid
to your Church;
She acknowledges you, she glorifies you,
she recognises no other God
or deliverer except you,
who laid down your life for her.

Accept the supplications of your people,
O Virgin Mother of God,
and intercede unceasingly with your Son,
that we who praise you may be freed
from peril and temptation.
You are, in truth, our ambassadress
and our hope.

JOHN OF DAMASCUS

He was born in Syria about 675 into a family which was first
in the service of the Byzantines and later of the Arabs. He
received a standard education and succeeded his father in the
office of governor of his native city. About 718 he embraced the
monastic life and then later became a priest, dedicating himself
immediately to preaching and the documentation of his works.
He died in 749, leaving an abundance of theological, ascetic
and liturgical works. The mysteries of Mary have been exalted
by him in homilies and hymns. The latter are to this day the
patrimony of the liturgical books of the Byzantine Church. With
John of Damascus, praise of Mary and the appeal for her intercession find memorable emphasis and they acquire a rare
perfection.

78. In you rejoices, O full of grace,
all creation, the company of angels
and all humankind.
O holy temple and spiritual paradise,
O pride of virgins.
Thanks to you, God took flesh
becoming a child,
he, our God, foremost of all ages.
Of your womb, he has made, in truth, a throne
and formed it greater than the heavens.
In you, O full of grace,
all creation rejoices.
Glory to you.

79. O most beautiful and sweetest maiden,
O lily, risen among the thorns,
grown on the royal and fertile root of David,
through you the sovereignty of priesthood is enriched.
O rose, appeared among the Jewish thorns,

who fills the world with divine perfume!
O daughter of Adam, O Mother of God!
Blessed be the womb from which you emerged.
Blessed the arms which carried you
and the lips that delighted in your innocent kisses,
the lips of your parents . . .
Today the salvation of the world begins!

80. Hail, Mary, sweetest daughter of Anne!
Love attracts me to you anew.
How can I describe your decorous bearing?
And your dress? And the beauty of your face?
And the prudent bearing in your prime of life?
Your dress was modest,
far removed from any extravagance,
your step is solemn, neither headlong nor flagging;
your conduct is thoughtful, lightened by youthful
    liveliness;
and greatest prudence towards mankind.
This was shown in the awe which surrounded you
at the unexpected meeting with the angel.
You were gentle and respectful towards your parents;
humble in spirit in the highest contemplation;
agreeable was the speech which came forth
    from your gentle soul.
In brief, naught else in you, if not the worthy
    dwelling place of God?
Rightly all generations call you blessed,
for you are the glory of the human race,
You are the pride of priests,
the hope of Christians,
the fruitful plant of virginity;
through you, in truth, the beauty of virginity
    is widespread.
Blessed are you among women and blessed is the fruit
    of your womb!

81. Today, we too, do linger
in your presence, O Sovereign!
I say again: Sovereign, Virgin Mother of God,
and let us bind our souls,
as to a steadfast and immovable anchor,
to the hope that you are for us.
Let us dedicate to you our spirit and our soul,
our body, our whole person.
We wish to honour you, as far as we are able,
with psalms, hymns and spiritual songs,
since it is impossible for us to honour you
according to your worth.
If, as a sign of the sacred word,
the honour which is offered to the servants,
bears witness to the love towards our mutual Lord,
can we not pledge ourselves
to render honour to you, Mother of your Lord?
Ought we not to pledge ourselves in every way?
Is it not desirable to our very breath,
from the moment that he gave us life?
In such a way we shall demonstrate
our love for our Lord.
What am I saying, for the Lord?
In reality, for those who piously honour your memory
the precious gift of your memory is sufficient;
it becomes the highest expression of everlasting joy.
Does not this joy, these gifts, fill
the one who has made in his soul
the dwelling for your sacred memory?

ETHIOPIC ANAPHORA

The Anaphora is a liturgical canon. The Ethiopic Anaphora which we quote is devoted entirely to Our Lady, and goes back to the 8th century. Its title is *Anaphora in honour of Mary*. We quote the final excerpt from the act of grace.

82. O Mary, immensity of heaven,
foundation of the earth,
depth of the seas, light of the sun,
beauty of the moon,
splendour of the stars in the heaven.
You are greater than the cherubim,
more eminent than the seraphim,
more glorious than the chariots of fire.
Your womb bore God,
before whose majesty man stands in awe.
Your lap held the glowing coal.
Your knees supported the lion,
whose majesty is fearful.
Yours hands touched
the One who is untouchable
and the fire of the divinity which is in him.
Your fingers resemble the glowing tongs
with which the prophet received the coals
of the heavenly oblation.
You are the basket for this bread of ardent flame
and the chalice for this wine.
O Mary, who nurtured in your womb
the fruit of oblaton,
we children of this sanctuary
we pray to you with perseverance
to guard us from the adversity which ensnares us
and as the measure of water
cannot be parted from the wine,
so let us not be separated from you and your Son,
the Lamb of salvation.

THE COPTIC MONTH TO MARY

The Christian Copts of Egypt dedicate a month, called Kiahk, to Our Lady. The liturgical book — dating from the 8th to the 9th century — is very lengthy indeed. It is called *Book of holy psalmody of the month of Kiahk arranged by the Fathers of the Coptic Church*. It includes prayers and hymns, doxologies and spiritual statements in honour of Mary. The text is in Coptic and Arabic. P. G. Giamberardini, well known Coptic scholar, has recently examined the book, giving long extracts in Italian translation. We quote two texts.

83. What shall I call you, O Virgin most holy,
now that you have borne the one impossible to reach,
the one who surpasses all things in the world?

What shall I call you, O city of the great king,
O embellished mansion of the king of kings?

What shall I call you, O Church of the First-born
and of celestial legions
who sing within it?

What shall I call you, holy and sublime ladder,
on whose summit is found the Lord
whom the angels glorify?

What shall I call you, O perfect spouse,
you who begot Emmanuel,
that is, Our Lord Jesus Christ?

What shall I call you, O propitious new heaven,
you who are the spiritual home of the chaste angels?

What shall I call you, O spiritual net,
you who extend to the catch of the fathers,
and all the company of prophets?

What shall I call you, to whom shall I liken you,
how shall I speak of you,
O holy Virgin and bearer of peace?

The Father bore witness to you,
for there was no-one like you;
for this you were chosen and sanctified.

The Son of the Father loved to dwell in you
and remained in your womb for nine months.

The Holy Spirit descended upon you
and sanctified you, O Virgin Mary!

What shall I call you, O propitious new heaven,
you have begotten God for us,
the One you have carried in your arms?

What shall I call you, O Zion, O Jerusalem,
since the joy of all the saints is found in you?

What shall I call you, O sublime mount of spices,
whereon dwelt our Saviour,
the Son of God?

What shall I call you, O tabernacle of Abraham,
who welcomed God and his chaste angels?

What shall I call you, O garment of the priest Aaron,
that one which, scarcely worn,
moved God to compassion for his people?

What shall I call you, O justice, O compassion,
those which meet together,
according to the voice of the prophets?

In truth, the Virgin is compassion,
and our Saviour is justice.

And to her who begot him,
and to him who saved us from our sins,
O Virgin Mary, hail!

84. O pure spouse, bearer of peace,
O Virgin and mother of the Word,
O Mary, O Mother of God;
plead with Christ for us, that he may show mercy

and intercede for our protection.
O Mary, Mother of God.
You O God, are the God of mercy;
enlighten us with your mercy;
and grant the demands of this spouse;
Mary, Mother of God.
Praise him, glorify him, O faithful people
for she is the Virgin:
Mary, Mother of God.
In your mercy, O Lord,
keep us and protect us:
thanks to the intercession of Our Lady:
Mary, Mother of God.
Blessed is your fruit, O Mary,
for you begot Christ,
remembered by the faithful.
O Mary, Mother of God.
Dwell in us at all times,
O Mary, Mother of God.
O You, One of the Trinity,
our Lord Jesus Christ;
you were Incarnate of the Virgin:
Mary, Mother of God.
O Saviour of all, O Life of all men,
dwell in us at all times:
Through Mary, Mother of God.
The God of our fathers,
the Lord of our fathers,
in you became flesh:
O Mary, Mother of God.
Behold, the Lord,
the King, the God of kingdoms,
was Incarnate in the Queen,
Mary, Mother of God.
We supplicate you, O our God;
grant us freedom and salvation
through the prayers of the Mother of God:
Mary, Mother of God.

Bless your inheritance,
grant us salvation and forbearance
through the intercession of the Holy One:
Mary, Mother of God.
Let all men glorify him!
Let all tongues glorify her!
who is the golden brazier,
the life of Christians,
the honour of the Virgin,
choice and pure gold:
Mary, Mother of God.
You, O Mary, are truly the protection
and the life of all men,
therefore we supplicate you at all times:
Mary, Mother of God . . .

THEODORE THE STUDITE

Born in Constantinople in 759, he became a Religious, together with two brothers and a sister. He was a vigorous defender of Christian doctrine and the cult of Icons. He became abbot of Studios (from which he was nicknamed Studite), was banished three times into exile, where he died in 826. His literary activity, complemented by his wonderful religious activity, has produced a lavish collection of letters, polemic and ascetic writings, homilies and epigrams in addition to a rich hymnography which is found in Byzantine liturgical books. There is attributed to him, to his brother and also to the Studite monks in general, the increase of Marian antiphons called Theotokia (to honour the Mother of God) and Staurotheotokia (to honour the Mother of God at the foot of the Cross).

85. O You, who penetrate the clouds and ascend to heaven,
who enter in the holy of holies with
exulting and praising voice,
deign to bless, O Mother of God, the whole earth.
With your intercession,
obtain for us a clean and temperate climate,
send us rain at the right time,
moderate the winds, keep the earth fertile,
keep away the barbarians
from the tranquillity of the Church,
steadfastness of the faith,
security of the nation,
and protect the whole Christian people.

JOSEPH THE STUDITE

He was a brother of Theodore the Studite, together with whom he experienced many vicissitudes. Born in 762, he followed his brother into the monastic life and in 807 became Metropolitan of Thessalonica. He died in exile in 832. His body, together with that of his brother Theodore, was taken to Constantinople in 844. The Greek Church numbers him among her saints. He bequeathed a great number of panegyrics, homilies and hymns, many of them honouring Our Lady.

86. Calm, O maiden most pure,
the wild storm of my soul,
for you alone showed yourself on earth to be
the port of all who set a course
through the perils of life.
You who gave birth to the Light,
brighten, O Pure Lady, the eyes of my heart.
You were given to us on earth
as protection, bulwark and boast.
You were given to us as a tower
and sure salvation, O maiden.
For this we no longer fear adversary,
we who devoutly glorify you.

H

THEOPHANUS THE MARKED ONE

Theophanus and his brother Theodore were two saintly brothers
of the Church of Jerusalem. Of a noble and pious family, they
became monks in the "Lavra" of St Saba. Transferred in 813 to
Constantinople, he defended orthodoxy against the iconoclastic
Emperors Leo the Armenian and Theophilus, suffering persecu-
tion, imprisonment and exile, resulting in Theodore's death in
844. Theophanus saw the restoration of the cult of Icons and
became Metropolitan of Nicea, where he died in 845. They were
nicknamed "The Marked Ones" for having had words cut on
their foreheads by the fire of their persecutors.
They bequeathed a rich collection of hymns, magnificently
honouring Our Lady. The texts which we quote are by
Theophanus.

87. The mystery hidden from the beginning
comes to light today and the Son of God
becomes the Son of man, so that,
assuming the limits of humanity
he could raise me above human nature.
Adam was deceived,
he could not become God as he imagined;
instead God becomes man to deify Adam.
Let creation rejoice, the earth dance,
for an archangel did appear
to the Virgin revered,
the bearer of joy — "Rejoice" —
where sorrow held sway.
Glory to you, our God, who for love became man!

88. Come, O festive angels,
let us prepare ourselves to dance
and to make the Church resound with songs
on the occasion of the deposition of God's Ark.

Behold: today heaven throws open its bosom
to receive her who brought forth the Great One;
the earth, receiving the source of life,
covered itself with blessings and beauty.
The angels make a choir with the Apostles
and watch over with reverence the Mother
of the King of life,
who passes from this life to the other.
Let us all kneel down before her and pray:
O Queen, do not forget those who are joined
to you by affinity and celebrate with faith
your holy dormition!

JOSEPH THE HYMNOGRAPHER

He was probably born in Salerno at the beginning of the 9th century and lived in Sicily from where he had to flee before the Arab invasion. He became a monk in Salonika and went to Constantinople about 840. Going on a mission to Rome he was captured by pirates. Released after long imprisonment, he returned to Constantinople where he devoted himself to the composition of hymns. He died in 886.

Joseph was considered the most celebrated and fruitful poet of sacred hymns contained in the liturgical books of the Greek Church. His hymns to Our Lady are numerous and collected together they form a *Mariale* (cf. PG 105, 983–1411). The text that we quote is an extract from the canon, which, together with the Acathistus hymn, forms the votive office of the Acathistus.

89. The archangel, beholding you, O chaste one,
   like a living book, sealed by the Spirit,
   exclaimed, addressing you:
   Hail, shelter of that joy
   which resolved the curse of the first mother.
   Hail, Virgin spouse divine,
   you who rehabilitates man and destroys hell.
   Hail, Immaculate, palace of the unique king;
   Hail, throne of the fire of the Omnipotent!
   Hail, the only one who has brought to flower the rose
   that does not wither;
   Hail, you who have borne the fragrant fruit,
   the king of all things.
   Hail, you, unacquainted with nuptials,
   and salvation of the universe.
   Hail, treasure of chastity;
   through you we have been raised from our downfall;
   Hail, Madonna, fragrant lily for the faithful,
   O sweet incense and precious balsam!

GEORGE OF NICOMEDIA

He was a writer of the 9th century, a disciple of Photius, who nominated him Metropolitan of Nicomedia (capital of Bitinia, now Imrid). He bequeathed hymns which are to be found in Greek liturgical books.

90. No impure hand dare touch
the one who is the living tabernacle of God.
Rather let the lips of the faithful proclaim
their rejoicing with the unceasing voice of the angel:
O pure Virgin, you are truly
the most exalted of all creatures!

O Virgin Mother of God, your soul
irradiates purity and beauty
and is filled with the celestial grace of God;
thus you ever illuminate with eternal light
those who acclaim you:
O pure Virgin, you are truly
the most exalted of all creatures!

O Virgin Mother of God, the virtue
of your prodigy surpasses words;
the Word perceived, in fact, in you
a body resistant to all sin;
since in the act of grace, it cries to you:
O pure Virgin, you are truly
the most exalted of all creatures!

O chaste one, the law has paradoxically
represented you as tabernacle and sacred chalice,
wonderful ark, veil and staff,
indestructible temple and threshold of God.
Thus it teaches us to exclaim:
O pure Virgin, you are truly
the most exalted of all creatures!

David, chanting, has prefigured you
describing you as the daughter of the king.
embellished with the beauty of virtue
and seated at the right hand of God.
Thus he, in truth rejoicing, exclaimed:
O pure Virgin, you are truly
the most exalted of all creatures!

Solomon, contemplating you in anticipation
as the dwelling of God, opened the gates for you,
you are the gateway of the king
and the living fountain engraved with a seal,
from which flows limpid water for us
which, with faith, we call:
O pure Virgin, you are truly
the most exalted of all creatures!

You bestow numerous gifts on my soul,
O Mother of God, causing life to flow to
the one who honours you as he should.
You then, forewarn, protect and keep
those who can acclaim you:
O pure Virgin, you are truly
the most exalted of all creatures!

GREEK VOTIVE OFFICE TO OUR LADY

The Greek Church, as a preparation for the Feast of the
Assumption on 15th August, is accustomed to sing each day
from 1st August, a Divine Office to Our Lady, called Paraclesis
or supplication. The recital, however, is not limited to the period
of the Assumption, but as the preceding rubrics say, it is recited
"in any ordeal or tribulation of the soul". The Office consists
of a canon, whose author was the monk Theostericatus (9th
century), the chant of the Gospel on the Visitation (Luke
2 : 39–56) and a great number of hymns of supplication to Our
Lady. Here are two of them.

91. We never cease to turn to the Mother of God,
    we who are oppressed by sin and misfortune;
    contrite, we prostrate ourselves and
    from the depth of our souls cry out:
    Help us, O Queen, stir yourself to pity for us;
    Hurry, we are about to succomb
    under the weight of sin.
    Do not send your servants back deluded,
    for you alone are our hope.
    O Mother of God, unworthy as we are,
    we will never cease to make known your power.
    If you had not been there to intercede for us,
    who would have freed us from so many dangers?
    Who would have kept us free till now?
    O Queen, we will not turn away from you,
    for you will always save your servants
        from all misfortune.

92. Do not abandon me, O Lady most holy,
    to the mercy of men;
    receive the supplication of your servant;

I am oppressed by anguish
and it is hard for me to resist the pressure of evil.
Wretch that I am! I have no defence
nor do I know where to take refuge;
opposed from all sides
I find no other comfort but in you.
O Queen of the world, hope and protection
of the faithful, do not scorn my supplication
but obtain for me that which I need.

PETER OF ARGUS

He was born in Constantinople at the end of the 9th century and became a monk. Elected Bishop of Argus Peloponnisos, he was famous for his great works of charity to the poor. He bequeathed several Marian homilies.

93. To us, therefore, your useless servants,
who with fear and longing dare to exalt you
and address our petitions to you, great Lady,
grant the remission of sins
and triumph over our enemies, visible and invisible;
grant healing to the sick,
grant to the healthy
a sense of gratitude and love for God,
to those who are divided grant unity,
to those who live in harmony with others
grant protection and stability,
to the disheartened and to the afflicted
grant pleasing consolation.
To those who are reluctant to follow the light of reason
send the light of divine grace.
Be a companion to those who journey,
steer with the one who is on the sea,
a support for him who falls,
a buttress for him who stands firm,
prosperity for him who has made good,
help for him who is in need.
Direct with assurance our whole life,
make us worthy of the splendour of the saints above
for, while we raise our hymns of praise
to you, our protectress,
we, together with them, render glory to your Son
    and God,
with the everlasting Father
and the Holy Spirit, the giver of life,
both now and always, for ever and ever. Amen!

I

10th CENTURY ANONYMOUS PRAYER

In Preparation for Communion

94. Blessed spouse of God, fertile earth
from which has sprouted without seed
the ear of salvation of the world,
make me worthy to eat it and save myself.

O Most Holy Altar, bearer of the Bread of Life
who out of compassion descended from heaven
and bestowed on the world a new life,
make me worthy to taste it and to live.

O Lady, welcome me with mercy
and give me your compassion;
keep me from blemish to receive
the precious pearl, and hallow me.

Mary, Mother of God, dwelling place
of the divine benevolence, through your prayers
make of me a chosen instrument
worthy of sharing
in the holy works of your Son.

O Holy Word of God, hallow all of me,
now that I prepare myself
for your holy mysteries,
through the prayers of your holy Mother.

O Pure One, full of divine grace,
you who brought forth Christ the Saviour,
I am about to draw near to the holy mystery;
I beg of you, purify me
from all blemish of body and soul!

On the point of receiving the Fire,
I shudder at being consumed like wax and grass.

Awesome mystery! How is it that I who am mire
am not destroyed
partaking of the Body and Blood of God?

God has taken substance from your immaculate Blood!
Thus the human race and the company of angels
sing glory to you, seeing with certainty
the Lord of the universe assume human form.

95. You, who gave birth to the source of immortality,
Most Holy Lady Mother of God,
light of the darkness of my soul,
O my hope and protection,
refuge, comfort and jubilation,
I thank you, for though unworthy,
you have made me a partaker of the immaculate body
and precious blood of your Son.

You who gave birth to the true light of the world,
enlighten the spiritual eyes of my heart.
You who gave birth to the source of immortality,
give life to me, dead through sin.

O merciful Mother of the God of love,
have pity on me and infuse in my heart
sorrow and repentance, humility in my thoughts,
and deliverance from the trials to which I am subjected.

Make me worthy, to my last breath,
to receive, without condemnation,
the sanctification that comes to me from your most pure
    mysteries
for the salvation of my soul and of my body.

Give me the tears of penitence and confession,
so that I can hymn my praise to you
and glorify you all the days of my life,
for you are blessed and glorified
for ever and ever. Amen!

FULBERT OF CHARTRES

A theologian of the Gallican Church and writer, he was Bishop of Chartres from 1007. Reports on his pastoral activities are scarce and fragmentary. He rebuilt the Cathedral of Notre Dame in Chartres, which had been destroyed by fire. He was a great defender of the rights of the Church against the arrogance of the nobility, and was an austere spiritual director. He wrote numerous sermons and tracts. In one of his sermons is found, probably confirming the popular piety of the times, the Invocation to Our Lady which we quote. He was born about 960 and died in 1028.

96. Holy Mary, succour the wretched,
helpthedisheartened,
put new heart into the feeble.
Pray for the people, intervene for the clergy,
intercede for all holy women.
May all those who honour your memory,
experience your generous help.
Promptly you attend to the voice of those who pray
to you
and satisfy the desire of each one.
Let your undertaking be diligent intercession
for the people of God.
For you have merited, O blessed One,
to bear the ransom of the world,
he who lives and reigns
for ever and ever.

THE HYMN "HAIL STAR OF THE SEA"

"Hail Star of the Sea" is the most popular Marian hymn. It is full of tenderness and images, consistent with the sentiments and affection, profoundly human, felt for Mary, which came to be invoked, as a point of orientation on the difficult sea of life. The hymn was attributed to various people: to Venantius Fortunatus († 601), to King Robert († 1031), and to St Bernard († 1153). It certainly dates from before 1000, because it already appears in manuscript no. 95 from the 10th century, preserved in the Swiss monastery of St Gall.

97. Hail, O star of the sea,
   glorious Mother of God;
   O Holy Virgin, Mary,
   O wide-open gate of heaven!

   The angel sent by heaven
   carries a message from God.
   You welcome him;
   changes then the destiny of Eve
   and peace smiles on the world.

   Break the chains of all oppression,
   proffer your light to those who cannot see,
   drive evil from every person,
   beg for each one all that is good.

   Let everyone experience that you are our Mother.
   Present our prayers to Christ
   and may he, who became your Son,
   with tender mercy receive them.

   Virgin sublime, sweet and beloved,
   free us from our guilt,
   make us humble and pure.
   Give us tranquil days,
   keep watch over our path
   until that day we shall meet your Son,
   joyfully in heaven.

INDEX

1. The Hymnographers

HYMNS ARRANGED ACCORDING
TO THEME

Prayers and hymns relating to the *Nativity of Mary:* nos. 79, 80.

Prayers and hymns exalting the *Annunciation:* nos. 5, 7, 17, 33, 34, 39, 50, 61, 67, 87, 89.

Prayers and hymns full of the fervour of waiting, in communion with Mary, for the *Advent* of Christ: nos. 16, 18, 19, 20, 71.

Prayers and hymns whose point is the mystery of the Incarnation, praise of Our Lady, Mother of God, and the *Birth* of the Redeemer: nos. 2, 4, 5, 8, 9, 12, 15, 21, 23, 37, 38, 39, 41, 42, 44, 45, 47, 48, 76, 78.

Prayers and hymns which record the *Passion of Christ* and Mary's sharing in the suffering of her Son: nos. 63, 64, 65.

Prayers and hymns which evoke and exalt the mystery of the *Assumption* of Mary to Heaven: nos. 53, 56, 57, 58, 85, 88.

Prayers and hymns turning back *to God and Christ* and to the *Intercessions* of Mary: nos. 10, 15, 16, 17, 18, 19, 20, 40, 45.

Prayers and hymns of *gratitude to Mary:* nos. 3, 21, 40, 41.

Prayers and hymns expressing feelings of *praise* and *joy:* nos. 1, 6, 7, 8, 11, 12, 13, 22, 23, 25, 26, 30, 31, 32, 33, 34, 36, 46, 47, 50, 52, 54, 55, 60, 61, 72, 77, 78, 79, 80, 81, 82, 83, 90.

Prayers with *invocations for help:* nos. 10, 14, 24, 27, 28, 29, 35, 51, 55, 59, 62, 66, 67, 68, 70, 71, 73, 74, 75, 77, 84, 85, 86, 91, 92, 93, 94, 95, 96, 97.

Contemplative extracts not expressed in the usual form of prayer: nos. 2, 5, 37, 38, 43, 44, 48, 49.

GLOSSARY

In the brief bibliographical notes and in the texts of this collected anthology, terms which are not in everyday speech have deliberately not been used. Nevertheless, there are some words which have been difficult to substitute. At other times, it was necessary to refer to generally little-known facts and characters of the biblical, theological and liturgical world. We give a short explanation of these terms.

ACATHISTUS: The term which, in Greek, means *I am not seated,* has given its name to the hymn which, in the Byzantine Church, is sung standing. The hymn, an example of a highly developed prayer, is a long poetical composition of 24 stanzas or strophes which honours the Virgin and the wonder of the Incarnation.

ANAPHORA: A term, peculiar to the Eastern Liturgy, corresponding to the Latin canon. It includes Consecration, and in particular, the raising of the Victim, offering it to God in sacrifice; it is, therefore, the central part of the Mass.

ARIANISM: Arius, a priest of Alexandria (4th century) of genuine ascetism, gave his name to Arianism, a false doctrine sustained with deliberate vagueness of language and interpretation which troubled the Church for some centuries: Arius stated that Jesus was a creation of the Father, hence, having had a beginning, is not God, but an intermediary between God and the world; an indefinite being, neither God in a full sense, nor Son of God in an adoptive sense, whose unique attribute, clearly affirmed, was to raise on high all creatures to a sphere between the eternal and the transient. With regard to the figure of Mary, she came to be recognised as the Mother of Jesus, but not as the Mother of God. This false doctrine was opposed by scholars, foremost among them Athanasius of Alexandria. At the Council of Nicea (325) Arianim was condemned and the divinity of Jesus and his equality with the Father was reaffirmed.

ARMENIANS: Armenia is a mountainous region of Asia Minor, whose territory is today part Russian, part Turkish and part Persian. It was evangelised in the 3rd century. Its most renowned "Catholicos" (this was the title of the delegate of the Bishop of Caesarea, responsible pastor for the area) was Nerses, poisoned by King Pap in 374 in order to separate the Armenian Church from Rome. The schism occurred in

551. The Monophysite Heresy then penetrated the schismatic Armenian Church. At the beginning of the 15th century, at the Council of Florence, a section of the Armenian Christians were reunited with Rome, conserving however, their own liturgical rite. The Armenian Liturgy could be considered as representing the oldest phase of Byzantine Liturgy. It used the classical Armenian language of the 5th century. In Italy, on the Island of San Lazzaro of Venice, there is still a community of Armenian Religious: Benedictine Mechitarists.

BYZANTINE: It refers to the city of Byzantium. While Rome remained the capital of the Western Roman Empire, Byzantium was made capital of the Eastern Roman Empire in 330, having, and keeping, the name of Constantinople from the name of its restorer, Constatine the Great. From then, with the split always deeper, the Eastern Empire and the Western Empire lead their own lives and had their own history, separate and different. While the Western Roman Empire started to decline from the 5th century, weakened by the Barbarian invasions, the Eastern Roman Empire (or Byzantine) still remained steadfast, even through intrigues, conspiracies and civil unrest until the end of the 11th century. From the 9th century there was a change in the concept of the Byzantines with regard to the Universal Church. The Pope began to be considered simply as the Patriarch of the West. Photius, Patriarch of Constantinople, brought Greek national pride into the ecclesiastical sphere. It was through this, that in the face of some real dissension with Rome, dialogue became ever more difficult and the schism was then inevitable (1054). The *Byzantine Liturgy,* already in use in the whole of Asia Minor in the 4th century, was arranged and reduced in form by St Basil the Great († 379). It was used widely in Syria, in Central Italy and in the Slav countries. In all these areas the liturgy soon developed local variants in language, music and formulae. The Byzantine Liturgy is complex and solemn and has retained many aspects of the Christian Liturgy of the first centuries.

CANON: Literally means principle, rule. In the Greek liturgy a part of the office of the ninth hour is so-called. In the Roman liturgy the central part of the Mass came to be called the canon, the most important part, which contains the formula of the Consecration. The Latin canon corresponds to the Greek anaphora.

CANONICAL HOURS: This is the name of the subdivisions of the recital of the Divine Office (or Breviary) in the Latin Church: office of reading, lauds, matins, midday hour (terce, sext, none) vespers and compline. The Divine Office is the consecration to God of the different hours of the day. The various parts constitute a *Liturgy of the Hours* and link up again with the Mass, keeping the more authentic and privileged expression of a Church that prays. All the hours have a similar pattern, consisting of psalms, hymns, readings from the Bible and the Fathers.

CONTAKION: A poetic composition of the Byzantine Divine Office, which outlines the theme of the feast of the day.

DEBORAH: A Hebrew prophetess. The Book of Judges refers to her in chapters 4 and 5. She was charged with judging the people and held her tribunal under a palm tree, passing judgement on religion and politics, on things both public and private. She led the people of Israel to freedom, fighting the Canaanite oppressors. Because of her dedication to the well-being of her people, some Fathers see in Deborah a prefiguration of Mary.

EXEGESIS: The term, which means the same as exposition and interpretation, is used to show ability to understand, translate and comment on old texts, particularly the sacred Books of the Bible.

FLEECE: The Book of Judges tells of the fleece, the hide of a sheep covered by wool. Gideon, judge of the tribe of Israel, begged this miracle of God: that for one night dew might fall on the fleece stretched out on the ground, leaving the surrounding earth dry; and on another night that the dew might wet the ground, leaving the fleece dry. All this happened, and it was for Gideon the proof of the heavenly blessing on the mission that God had charged him with, that of defending the Hebrews from their enemies.

GNOSTICISM: With this term from the Greek "gnosis-science" is suggested a movement of thought arising from the time of the Apostles, or probably even earlier, and developed in the 2nd and 3rd centuries, and in certain of its tendencies and its doctrines, surviving to this day (in France and Germany). However the convictions of the various gnostic sects are not united and the documents with which they can assert the true essence of gnosticism are few. It is nevertheless possible to sketch in broad outline a picture of the movement and common principles of all the sects. These are: the affirmation that the only way to salvation is knowledge. Jesus, sent by the Father to the world, revealed to mankind a lesson for salvation, but did not redeem mankind in the Christian sense. All creation is an emanation of God; between God and man there existed an intermediary (Demiurge) identified by some with the King of the Hebrews; through which came to be found an incommensurable distance between man and the Father; in man there is, therefore, a divine spark of varying degree, according to the person, depending on nature and not on the will of man. In the world there exist two opposing principles, good and evil, like light and darkness, a conception greatly developed in the Manichean sect. However one looks at ethics, gnostics hold opposing views; for some, a severe austerity of costume, for others, an unbridled debauchery because that which concerns the "material", which is in itself evil, does not touch the spirit and cannot corrupt it.

HOLY OF HOLIES: This was the name of the innermost part of the Temple of Jerusalem which protected the Ark of the Covenant under the wings of two cherubim.

HOMILY: The word, derived from the Greek, and which means conversation, familiar discourse, came to specify comment on the Sacred Scriptures, in particular on the Gospel of the day, during Mass. The homilies of some of the Fathers are well-known, Leo the Great, Ambrose, Augustine, John Chrysostom.

ICON: In a generic sense it means any religious picture, especially the one placed above altars. But current use reserves the term for sacred pictures of Eastern art, representing Christ, the Virgin or saints. Of Byzantine origin, the style and technique of Icons was then imported into Russia, where they attained a high degree of refinement. Icons exercised a profound influence through their hieratic expression and for the spiritual beauty which pervades them. At the beginning of the 8th century the cult of Icons in the East approached fanaticism and caused the arbitrary intervention of the Emperor Leo 3rd the Isaurian (726) who ordered their total destruction. The people, spurred by their faith, rebelled and the struggle was prolonged for about a century. They were persecuted and martyred. The Emperors and the ones who carried out the orders for the destruction of Icons are called Iconoclasts. Among the most stubborn defenders of the legitimate cult of images Germanus of Constantinople and John of Damascus are remembered.

JACOBITES: This is the name of Syrian Monophysites, followers of Jacob Baradaeus (6th century). They dedicated themselves to the reorganisation of the Monophysite Church dispersed in numerous sects, preaching, ordaining bishops and deacons, creating thus an independent hierarchy. In 1440 a part of the Jacobite Church united with the Catholic Church, then, with other groups which united themselves with Catholicism, they assumed the name of Syrian Malankarese.

LAVRA OR LAURAH This name, in Eastern monasticism, implies a group of anchorites who lived in separate huts, under the authority of one superior. The Lavra is an intermediate form between villages of hermits and a monastery in the strict sense. The Lavra of St Saba, in a wild, rocky desert between Jerusalem and the Dead Sea is famous. The Bishop and

Father of the Church, John of Damascus, lived there in the 8th century.

LEAH: Wife of the Biblical Patriarch Jacob. The Book of Genesis mentions her. She had many sons, among them Judah. The tribe of Judah gave the direct worldly lineage of the Messiah.

LITURGY: The word means, in Greek, a service to the people. In traditional religion liturgy also means religious rites with regard to acts of public worship. Catholic liturgy is the source and the culmination of the Church's worship. The formulae and rites are determined in order to maintain the faith and are an outward expression of it. Liturgy has assumed diverse manifestations, according to the places in which it was built up and elaborated; the Byzantine liturgy (Byzantine-slav, in use in the Russian Patriarchal Church; Ruthenian, in use in the Catholic Ukraine; Maronite; Armenian, etc.) and the Latin liturgy (Roman, the most widespread; Ambrosian, for the diocese of Milan and some adjoining places; The Rite of Lyons for the city of Lyons; Mozarabic for Toledo Cathedral; The Rite of Braga for the Portuguese city of Braga).

MARIALE: Collection of texts, hymns and prayers dedicated to Mary, Mother of God. The book is used for study, personal meditation and prayer.

MANUSCRIPT: In a generic sense it means any document whatsoever written by hand. It assumes specific significance when it is equivalent to a book written with a pen, or similar instrument, in an era long before the invention of printing. Be it on papyrus, parchment or card, the manuscript is an object of analysis and study, as one of the most important examples of the thought and civilisation of the past.

MARONITES: A Christian community of Syrian origin. The group was established around the monastery situated on the River Orente in Syria, a monastery dedicated to the monk St Maro, who died about 410. With the destruction of the monastery by Arabs, between the 10th and the 11th centuries, most of the monks and the faithful emigrated to Lebanon, founding the original Maronite community there and in Cyprus. The Maronite Church, which was initially dependent on the patriarch of Antioch, in the 8th century became autonomous, and notwithstanding the pressure of the patriarch on the community, resisted this, keeping its own patriarch, Syrian language and its own rites. In Lebanon today the Maronites still remain a religious and solid political bloc. The Catholic Maronite Rite derives from the Antiochene liturgy with modifications from the Latin Rite.

133

MEGALINARIA: Poetical composition, particularly in praise of Our Lady and the saints, belonging to the Byzantine Church.

MONOPHYSITISM: Heretical doctrine advocated by Bishop Eutyches (4th century) which, with the object of opposing the doctrine of Nestorianism, upheld that in Christ there was one nature, and that, divine. The precise meaning of Monophysite, a Greek word, is a single nature. Christ, according to Monophysites, is the true God, but is not simultaneously man. In him the human nature is as absorbed in that of the divine. The Monophysites were condemned at the Council of Chalcedon in 450. They survived afterwards for some centuries, and still survive, especially in the Egyptian Coptic Church (3 million believers) and in the Abyssinian Coptic Church (8 million believers).

MONOTHELITISM: A heresy of Monophysite derivation, which 'affirms that there is in Christ one single will, and not two, namely human and divine. It was stubbornly opposed by the learned bishop of Jerusalem, Sophronius, and was condemned at the 3rd Council of Constantinople in 680.

MOZARABIC: The term, derived from Arabic, means "arab-ized". It was the name given by the Moors of Spain in the Middle Ages, to their subjects and to the Christians living among them. The Mozarabic Christians assumed, in part, the language, the costume and the civilisation of the rulers, establishing a very remarkable arab-christian civilisation. The liturgy, too, assumed its own form, and under the name of *Mozarabic Rite* survived until the end of the 12th century. Today it exists only in Toledo Cathedral.

NESTORIANISM: A heretical doctrine formulated by Nestorius, Patriarch of Constantinople (elected in 428) who upheld that there were in Christ, two clearly separate and distinct natures, yet united in one single person; humanity and divinity existed side by side, each one keeping intact its peculiarities and modes of operation. The Nestorian doctrine left the impression that there was in Christ almost two persons, artificially joined together. Mary, as a result, was the Mother of Christ the man, not the Mother of God. The heresy, which had a fierce adversary in Cyril of Alexandria, was condemned by the Council of Ephesus in 431. Here Mary was solemnly proclaimed *Theotokos,* namely the Mother of God.

ORTHODOXY: In an objective sense, it is the whole truth propounded by faith; in a subjective sense, it is the acceptance of such truth on the part of individuals and of the Christian community, who as a result, are orthodox. Orthodoxy presupposes dogma, which is its object. Dogma exacts unconditional faith because God himself became the guarantor through his Word in his revelation of the truth which it propounds. He who was outside orthodoxy came to be called a heretic.

OSTRAKON : The Greek term means seashell, but by extension, it has come to mean anything which has a round appearance, like potsherds, crockery and other things. Particularly valuable are the potsherds used for writing on, be it by means of incision or with ink. In Egypt the use of ostrakons was systematic. On potsherds there were literary and religious texts, documents and letters. In Greece ostrakons were adopted to ban, by voting, some undesirable citizen. From this comes the term ostracism.

PAPYRUS : Plant of the sedge family, which grows luxuriantly on river banks and in marshy places. In ancient times it grew abundantly along the Nile and the Egyptians used it originally, with suitable workmanship, as writing material. Properly prepared, the page of papyrus is white, but with time it yellows and after centuries, the old papyri, appear a yellow opaque colour with grey tints. Papyrus was generally kept in scrolls (called volumes) but was also folded in four and sewn. Papyrus was used extensively as writing material until the 7th century A.D. and after the Arabian conquest of Egypt, it was replaced by parchment, more economical and practical.

PARACLESIS : An expression, which in Greek means comforter, became the title of a Divine Office which, especially in the Greek Byzantine Church, is celebrated on many occasions and above all, in preparation for the Marian Feast of 15th August. It consists of various prayers, and excerpts from Luke's Gospel and a canon, namely, a poetic text composed of nine odes.

PELAGIUS : A monk, probably born in Britain, lived in Rome, then in Africa and afterwards in Jerusalem, about the middle of the 4th century. Pelagius, relying too much on the hardened determination of the ascetics, attributed to man the full possibility of performing good and to keeping himself immune from every sin, even without the supernatural help of grace. Augustine and Jerome were enlightened opposers of this doctrine, condemned by Pope Zosimus in 418.

PRESBYTER : The name, given in the Acts of the Apostles, to the head of the Christian community. Its leader was Christ, from whom the presbyter derived all his authority. He performed the service of guidance in the external and internal edification of the community. In the Acts of the Apostles, the terms presbyter and bishop are used with equal significance. However, in the following centuries, the term presbyter indicated a simple priest.

REBECCA: Wife of Isaac and mother of Esau and Jacob, the narrative of her life occurs in Genesis. Shrewdly, she secured the rights of the firstborn for her favourite son Jacob and protected him from the vendetta of his brother Esau, who hoped for a similar inheritance of primogeniture. She was the bearer of divine blessing (as Paul said in his letter to the Romans, 9:10) and, in this way, was a prefiguration of Mary.

SARAH: Wife of the Patriarch Abraham. The Book of Genesis refers to her. Although she was advanced in age, she gave birth to Isaac, the promised son. And thus, she was the prefiguration of Mary.

STUDIOS: A monastery in the neighbourhood of Constantinople, named after its founder, the Consul Flavius Studios (433). The monks, called Studites, exercised a great influence on Byzantine religious life and civilisation. At Studios painting was developed, codices transcribed, hymns were composed and literature and sacred lore were developed. Theodore the Studite, a theologian of considerable distinction, introduced the Rule of St Basil to Studios in 826. With the fall of the Byzantine Empire, the monastery also declined. When Constantinople was conquered by the Turks in 1453 the monks were dispersed and the monastery turned into a mosque.

THEOPHANY: The name of a particular facet of the appearance of God. According to the Old Testament, man cannot see God without dying. Nevertheless, Holy Scripture tells how God appears, either in human form or in a way comprehensible to man.

THEOTOKOS: A Greek word with which the Council of Ephesus proclaimed and exalted the divine Motherhood of Mary, contested by Nestorius. Literally means *Mother of God*.

TROPARION: An original term from the Byzantine Liturgy. It means an unofficial text which was inserted in the liturgical texts to give solemnity to the liturgical action. It has different names, according to the order of the Divine Office. Troparion is also the name of the hymn sung during communion in the Mass.

VULGATE: Latin version of the Bible, main work of St Jerome, accepted by the Church at the beginning of the 5th century. Vulgate means that it can be read by all. The Council of Trent declared the Vulgate "authentic".